# Cruising
## the Columbia
## and Snake Rivers

by Sharlene P. and Ted W. Nelson
and Joan LeMieux

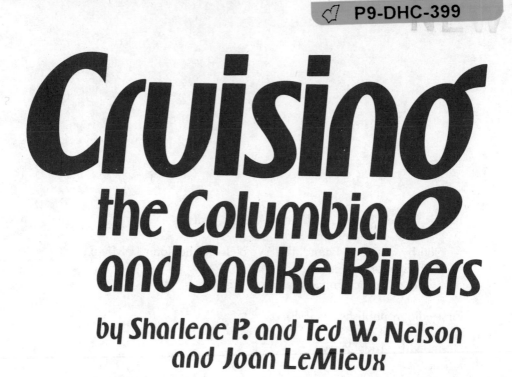

SECOND EDITION,
REVISED AND ENLARGED

Pacific Search Press

Pacific Search Press, 222 Dexter Avenue North
    Seattle, Washington 98109
© 1986 by Sharlene P. and Ted W. Nelson and Joan LeMieux.
    All rights reserved
    Printed in the United States of America

First edition published in 1981

Designed by Judy Petry

Photographs are by Sharlene P. Nelson and Joan LeMieux except
those by the following:
    U.S. Army Corps of Engineers (pages 17, 22, 33, 41, 53, 54,
        60, 62, 73, 78, 79,)
    Port of Cascade Locks (page 84)
    Oregon Department of Transportation (pages 45, 89)

Cover: *Sailboats on the Columbia River with Mount Hood in the background
(State of Oregon Tourism Division).*

**Library of Congress Cataloging-in-Publication Data**

Nelson, Sharlene P.
    Cruising the Columbia and Snake rivers.

    Bibliography: p.
    1. Boats and boating—Northwest, Pacific—Guide-books. 2. Snake
River (Wyo.-Wash.)—Recreational use—Guide-books. 3. Columbia
River—Recreational use—Guide-books. 4. Fishing—Snake River
(Wyo.-Wash.)—Guide-books. 5. Fishing—Columbia River—Guide-books.
6. Northwest, Pacific—Description and travel—1981—Guide-books.
7. Snake River (Wyo.-Wash.)—Description and travel—Guide-books.
8. Columbia River—Description and travel—Guide-books. I. Nelson, Ted
W. II. LeMieux, Joan. III. Title.
GV776.N76N44   1986                    917.95                    85-25978
ISBN 0-931397-04-9

# Contents

# Acknowledgments

There are many who have added to our knowledge and to our perspective of the inland waterway. We thank them all and wish we could name them all, but the list would go on and on. We do want to single out for our special thanks and appreciation: Sandy Dillard, Gary Olson, Tina and Jim O'Bannion, Kay Metz, Phyllis Knutson, Kay Peutz, Morely Paul, Jon Englund, Gary Cassidy, Dave Nicklous, Mel Lebeck, the U.S. Coast Guard at Kennewick, the U.S. Army Corps of Engineers at Walla Walla and Portland, and the marina operators. And thanks to tugboat captains Howard Everman and Loren Brooks, who shared their years of experience on the rivers; and to Jim Attwell, historian, and Harvey Steel, archeologist, who shared their years of research.

# Introduction
## to Second Edition

Being boaters and having experienced the challenges and pleasures of sailing the inland waterway of the Columbia and Snake rivers, we originally wrote this book for boaters. We described opportunities for those wanting to cruise the full 465 miles from the mountains of Idaho to the Pacific or for those wanting to sample only a short stretch. Since publication of the first edition, we found that the book also appeals to fishermen and to travelers who follow the roads that parallel the shores of the waterway.

This revised edition has been augmented to aid boaters as well as others who enjoy the rivers and want to learn more about the environs and history.

For boaters, we have updated the status of marinas. More of them now pump diesel. One marina closed, two new ones opened, three changed names, and some now offer more services.

For fishermen, there is a new chapter on sport fishing. Locations of fishing spots and of ramps to launch small boats are noted in the cruise chapters.

Because roads skirt the Columbia from the Tri-Cities in eastern Washington to the Pacific—about two-thirds the length of the inland waterway—road travelers like boaters can enjoy and see the places mentioned in the book. There are watermelon stands in Umatilla, many riverside parks like the one at Maryhill, a visitor's center at The Dalles Lock and Dam, the historic town of Skamokawa, a maritime museum in Astoria, and more. Those following the roads can also learn about the history and geology so interwoven with the rivers.

Should the river look inviting, and you want to park your car or bicycle to take a cruise, we have included a listing of river cruises. For those wanting to stop for a night, we have included a list of bed and breakfast establishments. For the boater, two of these are within walking distance of a marina or moorage.

The early history described in the first edition requires no revision, but information about the last five years does. The second powerhouse at Bonneville Lock and Dam was completed as was a second visitors' center located on the Washington State side. A new fish hatchery, which raises steelhead trout, and rainbow trout, and fall and spring

Chinook, was built on the Snake River at Lyons Ferry between 1981 and 1984. New vessels can be seen plying the waterway. The stern-wheeler *Columbia Gorge* was launched at Cascade Locks. Like a scene from the steamboat era a century ago, you can come aboard and ride on this replica of a sternwheeler. Exploration Cruise Lines began its summer cruises on the inland waterway in 1981. Wind surfers discovered the winds of the Columbia Gorge and now hold international competitions near Hood River.

Whether your view is from the river or from the road, we hope this book will enhance your experience along the inland waterway of the Columbia and Snake rivers.

# Prologue
# to a Waterway

Cruising the Columbia-Snake Inland Waterway offers a variety of experiences unlike any found on other waters of the West Coast. Its 465 miles begin on the Snake River at Lewiston, Idaho, and Clarkston, Washington, and will take you through varied and spectacular geography. The eastern segment includes semiarid and desertlike landscapes. The western segment cuts through a deep, timbered gorge, skirts Mount Saint Helens, then enters the Pacific below a mist-shrouded coastal headland.

Once a passage of pools and rapids, the waterway is now a series of stair-stepped lakes. Its system of eight dams with locks was completed in 1975 when the last dam, Lower Granite Lock and Dam near the Washington-Idaho border, was constructed and its gates closed, causing the waters behind them to rise and cover the shallows and rapids the last thirty miles of the inland waterway. The dams are multipurpose and were built by the U.S. Army Corps of Engineers. All provide hydroelectric power; some provide flood control and irrigation. At some dams, such as Bonneville on the Columbia, you can tie up and go ashore to watch turbine generators produce electric power or watch migratory fish swim up the fish ladders.

The combined waters through which these cruises will take you had their source in a basin of nearly 260,000 square miles. The Columbia begins in glacier-fed streams deep in the Canadian Rockies. The Snake rises near Jackson Hole, Wyoming, and lesser rivers and streams from Nevada, Utah, and Montana contribute to the flow.

From Lewiston to tidewater the waterway drops 730 feet; its steepest descent occurs through the four dams on the 140 miles of the

Snake. The last of the four dams on the Columbia is located 145 miles from the river's mouth.

Although the rapids are gone, cruising the waterway still offers challenges to boaters. "Locking-through" dams requires an alert skipper. Depths behind the dams are not affected by the moon as tides are, but levels may drop when water is released to generate electricity to meet power demands as far away as Los Angeles. Channels are narrow in some segments, and depths outside the main channel are often shallow, so navigation aids require special attention. Charts are mandatory for safety and depth-sounders are helpful.

The region's climate produces interesting combinations of wind and water activity. Steady summertime onshore winds in the lower reaches rival those of San Francisco Bay. Days in the eastern reaches can be warm and tranquil, punctuated by fierce westerlies, hard squalls, and an occasional dust storm. Fogs thick enough to obscure channel markers are infrequent, but they do occur in late fall and

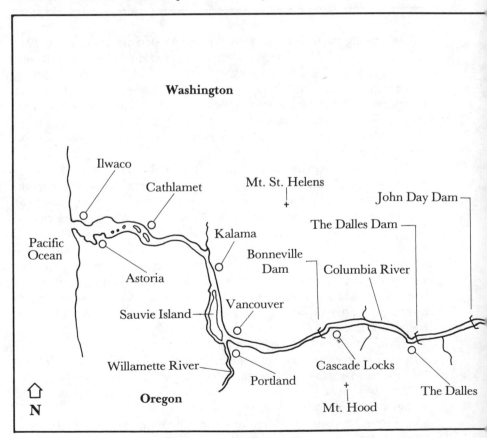

*Do not use for navigation.*
*See cruise maps for NOAA Nautical Chart numbers.*

winter, mainly in the western segment.

The waterway's spectacular settings are equaled by the contributions of its rivers to Pacific Northwest history. The continent's first peoples knew the rivers and their tributaries well. Eight thousand years ago men hunted in the rolling hills of the Palouse above the Snake. Later, the buffalo hunters of the plains rendezvoused with the fishermen of the coast at the river's "Long Narrows" to trade, gamble, and feast on the river's salmon bounty.

The Chinese may have known of the Columbia as early as A.D. 640 when, according to legend and some documented fact, a Buddhist monk named Hwui Shan crossed the western Pacific from his home in China. Later, geographers and adventurers conjured up a great "River of the West" that supposedly connected the Atlantic with the riches of the Pacific Coast and the Far East. In 1592, Juan de Fuca claimed that such a river existed on the western shore near forty-eight degrees latitude. An obscure nomad, Jonathan Carver, suggested the existence

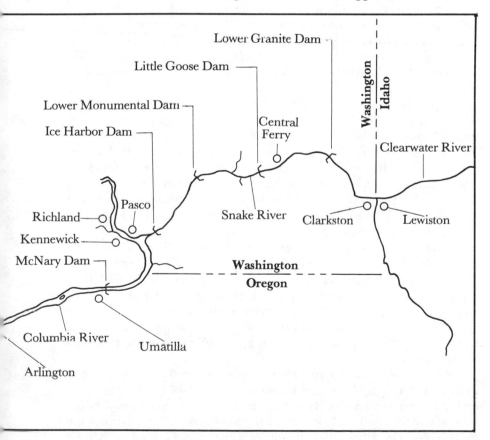

of a river "Origan" to George Rogers as he struggled through eastern Canada's Northwest Passage in 1766.

The first tangible evidence of the Columbia's existence was discovered by the Spaniards in their efforts to extend their domain northward from California. In 1775, Bruno Heceta encountered the river's strong westward current and muddy waters during his explorations. He named the area San Rogue but proceeded south without further investigation. Thirteen years later an English officer, Captain John Meares, in command of a Portuguese vessel, looked for Heceta's San Rogue. When he could not find it, he named Cape Disappointment to commemorate his failure.

By then, empires were taking shape and national territories were being staked. Lucratve business ventures were foreseen if the "River of the West" could be found. Captain George Vancouver, heir to Captain Cook's command, searched unsuccessfully for the river's mouth in April 1792.

The first modern discovery of the Columbia was left to the American Captain Robert Gray out of Boston, in search of pelts for the Orient trade. On 11 May 1792 he crossed the bar in his sloop, the *Columbia Rediviva*. For several days, Gray explored the river's estuary, then recrossed the bar and turned north for a chance encounter with Captain Vancouver.

Upon hearing of Gray's discovery, Captain Vancouver hurried to the river and on 20 October 1792, Lieutenant William Broughton was dispatched across the bar in the small armed tender, *Chatham*. Vancouver directed Broughton to explore the river in the name of the British Crown. In the *Chatham's* cutter and gig, Lieutenant Broughton rowed and sailed up the Columbia to the lower reaches of the Columbia Gorge. In his journals, he gave careful accounts of the lower river and named points familiar to us today—including Mount Hood, Warrior Point, and Puget Island.

The river's best-known explorers were William Clark and Meriwether Lewis. Near the end of their overland trek, they reached the Snake River near present-day Lewiston in October 1805. They reached the Pacific Ocean almost two months later, following the same course we describe here. On your cruise along the waterway, you will encounter the same grandeur so vividly documented by Lewis and Clark, and later encountered by trappers, settlers, gold-diggers, and steamboaters.

In this book, we describe eleven cruises along the waterway. The first cruise starts at Clarkston, Washington, and Lewiston, Idaho, and takes you down the Snake River to Central Ferry. Cruises two through nine assume a continued descent of the inland waterway. Cruises ten and eleven describe different routes from the Columbia River's estuary. While the consecutive cruises assume a steady descent of the rivers, they need not be taken that way. Each cruise describes a separate part of the waterway. Boaters can enter the rivers at many different points (we mention some launching locations) to visit or cruise any portion of the 465 miles of navigable water. The cruises can obviously be combined, or a portion of a cruise can be accomplished in a day with a late evening return.

The longest cruise is from Central Ferry on the Snake to the Tri-Cities, a distance of about eighty statute miles. The other cruises are from twenty-five to sixty statute miles. The endless combinations of winds and water, locking-through times, your boat's capabilities, and the interests of the skipper and crew will produce a wide range of travel times over a given stretch of water. The travel time estimates we show are intended to be only a gauge. The river miles from the mouth of the Columbia and the mouth of the Snake are shown on the schematic charts to help you plan your schedule. These are in statute miles, and can be correlated with the NOAA charts you will want to use.

Amenities of interest to boaters are described for each cruise, but information should be used with care. During the five-year span between our initial research and research for this revision, we found many facilities improved, others gone, and new ones built. Changes occur, so an establishment mentioned now may not be there next year.

The inland waterway has been relatively untouched by ongoing eruptions of Mount Saint Helens. The only part affected to date is the area around the mouth of the Cowlitz River, located in the lower reach of the Columbia. Following the first major eruption on 18 May 1980, a flood of mud and debris spilled from the Cowlitz into the Columbia. The silt spread upstream and downstream over a 10-mile stretch of the 465-mile-long inland waterway. The volume was large and temporarily closed this short portion of the main channel to ocean-going freighters. Although pleasure boating has been affected on the Cowlitz, it has not been hindered on the Columbia, which flows at the closest point, about 40 miles west of Mount Saint Helens.

Before discovering the Snake and Columbia, we had boated the blue waters of California, Washington's Puget Sound, and the brown waters of North Carolina's Pamlico River. We found that this western inland waterway presents challenges and opportunities not found elsewhere. We hope you enjoy it as much as we do.

# Cruise
# One

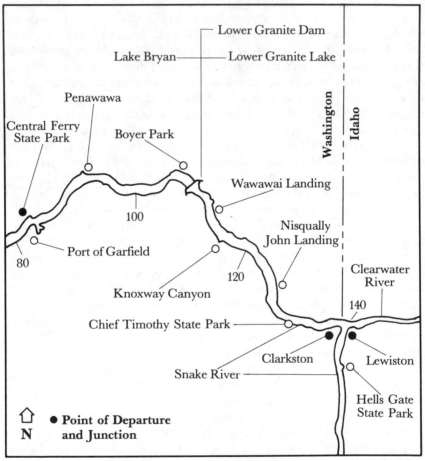

Lower Granite Dam

Lake Bryan — Lower Granite Lake

Penawawa

Washington | Idaho

Central Ferry
State Park

Boyer Park

Wawawai Landing

Nisqually
John Landing

100

Port of Garfield

80

Clearwater
River

120

Knoxway Canyon

140

Chief Timothy State Park

Clarkston

Lewiston

Snake River

Hells Gate
State Park

N ● **Point of Departure
and Junction**

*Do not use for navigation.*
*Use NOAA Nautical Charts 18548 and 18547*

# Lewiston-Clarkston to Central Ferry

**Point of departure:** Lewiston, Idaho; Clarkston, Washington

**Course:** Snake River via Lower Granite Lake and Lower Granite Lock and Dam with a vertical drop of 100 feet to Lake Bryan behind Little Goose Lock and Dam

**Stops:** Chief Timothy State Park, Knoxway Canyon, Boyer Park and Marina, Central Ferry State Park

**Length of cruise:** approximately 60 statute miles from Lewiston-Clarkston to Central Ferry

**Duration on power:** 1 day

**Duration on sail:** 2 days

**Overnight moorage:** Chief Timothy State Park, Boyer Park and Marina, Central Ferry State Park

**Junction point for Cruise Two:** Central Ferry State Park

# Canyon Walls

The Clearwater and Snake rivers merge in a valley on the Idaho border. The Clearwater flows from the east along the base of high, grassy hills. The Snake, now quiet after its plunge through Hells Canyon, flows from the south through low rolling hills and separates the communities of Lewiston, Idaho, and Clarkston, Washington. Beneath the grassy hills the Clearwater loses its identity as it spills into the silt-colored waters of the Snake. Here the Snake turns west to begin its descent through canyon walls and the Palouse country of Washington. This juncture forms the highest point of the inland waterway.

Uninterrupted passage the full length of the waterway has been possible only since the completion of Lower Granite Dam in 1975. This is the first dam you will lock-through, about thirty miles downstream. Since the dam's completion, commercial, private, and cruise vessels can sail from the Pacific to the mountains of Idaho. In response to increased waterway traffic, the ports of Lewiston, Clarkston, and Whitman County have grown, and the first phase of a new marina, Red Wolf Marina at Clarkston, opened in the spring of 1985.

Even though the white water thrills have been covered by slack water, the miles of river winding through steep canyon walls are still there to enjoy. Following the lower Snake River to its confluence with the Columbia River, you will lock-through four dams and drop almost four hundred feet along the 140 miles—the most rapid descent on the inland waterway.

One of the things we enjoyed most when sailing the Snake is the solitude. In spring or fall you may not pass another boat or see any sign of civilization for miles. You should have everything you will want on board before leaving Lewiston-Clarkston, since you will not find grocery and gas stops around each bend in the river.

There are two large marinas on the lower Snake. One is Boyer Park and Marina, just below Lower Granite. The other, Lyons Ferry Marina, is about fifty miles farther downstream, and is a stop on the second cruise. Both are well equipped for boaters' needs with moorage, supplies, and picnic areas. Unlike the San Juan Islands in Washington, where favorite anchorages are known to countless boaters, the bays at canyon mouths and inlets carved into a sandy bank of the Snake are largely untested.

For those with trailerable boats, many ramps, parks, and parking areas are located on the lakes behind the dams. Most parks have been built and are maintained by the U.S. Army Corps of Engineers, the agency that constructed the dams. The lakes offer a variety of places for swimming, water-skiing, fishing, or just loafing. Some boaters decide

*Sculpture marks the entrance to Lewis and Clark Center in Lewiston*

to put in on one lake to spend a day or two without having to lock-through a dam.

This cruise takes you through one dam, Lower Granite, to Central Ferry, about fifty-six miles downstream from Lewiston-Clarkston. You can divide the trip into one or two days, depending on your preference for speed or for leisure. Remember to allow time to lock-through the dam.

Lewis and Clark, on their descent of the same route in 1805, left their horses in care of the Nez Perce Indians and canoed down the Clearwater and onto the Snake. When the facing towns were settled years later, they were named in honor of these early explorers. The settlement of Lewiston began quite by accident. When gold was discovered upstream on the Clearwater in 1860, thousands rushed overland from western regions. The waterway was considered a quicker and more efficient means of travel, however, so a sternwheeler was engaged to carry freight and men up the Snake to the gold country. Len White, a riverboat captain, brought the first steamboat up the Clearwater. After steering beyond the confluence with the Snake, he was unable to find a landing. Returning to a sandbar near the Snake, he unloaded his freight and passengers, and Lewiston began. For awhile it was known as "Ragtown," and was the capital of Idaho Territory from 1863 to 1864.

Clarkston began as a ferry crossing for Idaho-bound prospectors. Until the 1860s, there was little settlement in what was first called "Jawbone Flats." The village went through several name changes before it became Clarkston in 1900.

Today Lewiston has a population of 31,000 to Clarkston's 7,000. The towns are in different states and separated by a river, but a bridge unites them, and they share services, employment, and cultural events. Though the valley itself is unforested, most of the local industry has some connection with wood products from the timber that begins twenty miles away in Idaho.

Trailerable boats can be launched from several good ramps with small docks along the Clarkston Greenbelt or the Lewiston Levee Parkway. These waterfront strips are landscaped and have hiking, jogging, and bike paths. If you intend to launch a large boat, you must get assistance from a crane company in either town.

Overnight moorage is available in Clarkston at the Red Wolf Marina or in Lewiston at the Hellsgate Marina. Hellsgate, located four miles up the Snake River above the highway bridge, adjoins a state park, where you might choose to spend more than a day. The park extends to the river where you can swim, fish, or water-ski from the docks. A playground, picnic spots, and restrooms with showers are also available. Bike rentals, as well as excursion rides for the 180-mile round trip into Hells Canyon, can be arranged. The marina has a boat ramp, gas, water, hookups, and groceries.

One difficulty with passage to the marina from the confluence of the rivers is the highway bridge, which has a clearance of ten feet. Since it is on navigable waters, there is a lift span. To have it opened, notify the Interstate Bridge Control at (208)746-0663 or on Channel 1. The bridge will be opened on request at the hours of 6:00 and 10:00 A.M. and 3:00, 7:00, and 9:00 P.M. if they are notified two hours in advance.

If you have to wait below the bridge, tie up at Greenbelt Park, which is near the Corps office just below the bridge in Clarkston. This is also a good place to stop for all supplies except gas—unless you want to carry it. A restaurant, supermarket, and gas station are a short two blocks away. This park is for day use only. If you want to moor overnight, there is the Red Wolf Marina down river in Clarkston. They pump gas and diesel, operate a boat lift, and are within walking distance of a supermarket.

Before starting on your trip you may want to swing a short distance up the Clearwater. The railroad bridge is left open most of the time, and tugs go beyond it to pick up barges of containers, paper products, and grain. You should keep to the north side of the channel. From here you look south across the levee that protects Lewiston. The tops of red brick buildings downtown appear above the levee; graceful older homes stand among trees on ridges above. In the spring, the eastern hills where the Clearwater flows are like a lush green carpet. Turning the bow down river, you nose into the Snake and pass the sandy beaches of Clarkston. You are now en route down the inland waterway.

A new bridge, which on the charts reads "under construction," is now completed. Connecting Clarkston with the Port of Wilma, Whitman County, its span is high and passable. The bridge's official name is Red Wolf Crossing Bridge, but it is known locally as the "someday bridge," since it was so long in the planning. The port stands by itself on the north shore on a bench of land, separated by a highway from the steep mountain beyond. Signs of its increasing activity include cranes, a chip pile, and decks of logs. Again, the logs seem out of place, since all the surrounding hillsides and mountains, unless planted with grain, are covered with bunch grass, sage, and cactus.

Almost immediately you begin to feel as if you are entering a deep canyon. Down river shoulders of mountains hunch up against the sky two thousand feet on either side. On the upper reach of this cruise, these great towering mountains seem to enclose the river, leaving only a slit of sky overhead. The canyons taper down and open up below Lower Granite but reappear again and again almost the entire length of the lower Snake.

Near Silcott Island the river turns, then disappears behind the mountains. On this island to the south is Chief Timothy State Park, which was opened in May 1980 and is the first park on the lower Snake River. A bridge crossing on the south side makes the park accessible by car. For a lunch or an overnight stop the park has all the amenities except shade—it will be a few years before the new trees grow enough to cast large shadows. You can, however, cool off in a protected swimming area. Facilities also include a launch ramp with a small dock, picnic tables, trailer hookups, a playground, restrooms, and changing rooms.

You will find deep water for anchorage on the southeast side of the island. As you approach it from up river, the entrance and the depth may look questionable. However, during construction of the park, a large tug with a draft of nine feet pulled in here and maneuvered in the waters with ease. You can drop an anchor or tie to the buoys.

The park is named for Chief Timothy, a Nez Perce Indian and a friend of the early white settlers. He saved a child during the Whitman Massacre, and later saved a detachment of soldiers by finding a retreat for them in 1858. His daughter, Jane, married John Silcott, who ran a ferry across Alpowa Creek, which empties into the Snake near the island. When prospectors were unable to find gold here, Jane led them to the first discovery near the Clearwater.

To commemorate the contribution that Lewis and Clark made when they traversed this part of the country, a new Lewis and Clark Interpretive Center built by the Washington State Parks and Recreation Commission was opened at the park in the fall of 1980. It is the newest of three centers, all located along the inland waterway. One is at Sacajawea Park at the confluence of the Snake and Columbia, the other at Fort Canby State Park, at the mouth of the Columbia overlooking the Pacific Ocean.

Turning north the river moves through precipitous cuts revealing the lava flows that covered this region. These formations of Columbia River basalt will be your companions for the next 400 miles, but their height and character will change almost constantly. Some are sheer, deeply indented walls, some are crumbling, some are softened by winds and rains and support grass, trees, and wildflowers. As the lower Snake cuts through these lava flows, it takes many twists and turns, and there are few places where one sees a broad or long view of the river for the next 120 miles.

The waters here are deep, down to 129 feet in some spots, and the current is barely perceptible. Under sail in a light breeze you are aware of the stillness broken only by the song of a meadowlark, or the occasional passing car on the north shore road. Powerboaters might consider turning off the motor and drifting for awhile to enjoy the silence.

Ridges high above run parallel with the river, then give way, folding back into wide gullies like huge amphitheaters. Trails run along some of the cliffs, and when we saw animals grazing along the toe-edge of one we thought we might be watching mountain sheep. But we pulled out our binoculars only to see cattle munching on grass, apparently unconcerned with the long, steep drop below them.

About fifteen miles from Lewiston, next to the highway on the north shore, there is a small boat launch and dock with picnic tables. Called Nisqually John Landing, it is similar to two other landings, Blyton and Wawawai, farther down river. People launch their boats here for a day of fishing or water-skiing.

This landing takes its name from a Nisqually Indian called Squally John. As a young man, he had fled from his tribe on Puget Sound after a fight with the medicine man. In 1848 he settled in a cabin once used by fur trappers, and was eventually given a patent for seventy-eight acres on the river. Records indicate that Squally John was one hundred years old when he died.

Because the water behind Lower Granite Dam filled in canyons, beaches are few. On the south shore there are two or three small grassy spots where a small runabout could be pulled in. At Knoxway Bay, eight miles from the dam—near day marker number ten—is a small Corps of Engineers park with a dock and boat access only. The park is located at the bottom of a canyon on a small apron of land sparsely dotted with trees.

At nearby Knoxway Canyon, a grain pipeline once descended this break to a warehouse and steamboat landing that stood on a wide beach. The pipeline is gone, and remnants of the landing and warehouse are under deep water.

The dams on the Snake are named for a geographic feature near each dam's location. About two miles below Knoxway Canyon you approach the one for which Lower Granite Dam is named—an outcropping of granite in a mass of basalt at Granite Point. In the late 1800s, fifty men worked here blasting rock that was then hauled down river for construction projects, including the custom house at Portland and the Cascade Locks.

Down river and around the bend on the north shore, you will find Wawawai Landing and Wawawai Bay County Park. The park, once an Indian village site and later a homestead, was completed in 1980. It was planned and landscaped above a bay to include locust trees planted by a pioneer. Early spring is a good time to fish in the bay for bluegill, perch, smallmouth bass, crappie, and bullheads. There are picnic tables, a playground, camping for a fee, restrooms, and a small swimming area marked by a sign reading "Swim at your own risk." Small boats can usually access the park from the inlet, but it may be boomed off to keep out floating debris and powerboats.

Today, on the incline above the park where the highway twists away from the river, the land is bare and the old orchards are gone. It is difficult to imagine that this location was once the busiest fruit-shipping port on the lower Snake River.

Indians who lived here for thousands of years called this place Wawawai, meaning "talk-talk," or council grounds. When the first pioneers arrived in the late 1800s, they settled on the broad areas of land now submerged and kept the Indian name. Orchards of cherries, apricots, peaches, and plums once flourished along the banks. At its peak the town boasted packing houses, a cookhouse, and a bunkhouse for pickers, a store, schoolhouse, and homes.

Down river from the park, you can tell, even without turning the bend, that you are approaching Lower Granite Dam. Several miles upstream from this and other dams, large towers strung with power lines appear to stalk across the hilltops headed for an unknown destination.

The navigation lock at Lower Granite is located in the center of the dam. Observe the locking-through procedure described in the chapter on navigation. If there is a long wait to lock-through, you can tie up at Offield Landing on the south shore. Stay clear of the restricted area. Marked by buoys at all dams, this area is above the spillways and powerhouse where the current moves faster.

Boyer Park and Marina, a mile below the dam, is a green oasis beneath summer-browned hills, headquarters for powerboat races,

*Lower Granite Lock and Dam*

home of the Washington State University crew, and a water playground for sunbathers, swimmers, skiers, and fishermen. People from long distances arrive at the park by car, boat, and plane (an airstrip is adjacent to the park).

Both the park and the marina, open seven days a week from mid-March until the first weekend in November, have all the necessary amenities, from laundry facilities to a launch ramp, to accommodate boaters for anything from a short fuel stop (including diesel) to a several days' stay. A fee is charged for overnight or longer. A few basic groceries such as bread, milk, and snacks can be purchased in an attractive wood building above the marina. The same building houses a restaurant, The Brass Compass Inn, serving hamburgers to full course meals, and a lounge offering beer and wine.

If the surroundings entice you to make an extended stay, you might consider a walk up the road past an old farmhouse and cherry trees to Lower Granite Dam. You can walk across the top of the dam to view its workings, a fish ladder, and other boats locking-through. In the evening, when activity has quieted and the summer daytime temperatures of ninety to one hundred degrees have cooled, you may want to mingle with other vacationers around a campfire on the beach.

As you leave or pass Boyer Park, avoid the shoal below the marina entrance near the south shore. It is now marked with a black buoy. Locally, the shoal is called "Prop Island." Until it was marked, powerboats sped across the top, banging their props hard enough to require repairs or replacement.

You are now cruising on Lake Bryan, the thirty-seven-mile-long pool behind Little Goose Lock and Dam. Little Goose is a run-of-the-river dam; the amount of water stored is small compared with the amount that passes across the dam. Depending on the season and river flow, water takes one to eleven days to move through this lake. During releases for the power plant, the lake can drop five feet—something to be aware of here and on other pools or lakes. Anchor in good depths, so that if the water is drawn down, you will not be left high and dry. If you are, just wait for the water to rise. Unlike tides that swing at known intervals, rising water in these lakes may take more than a few hours, possibly a day or two.

One skipper was trapped not by low water but high water. He negotiated his small sailboat under a railroad bridge into a bay during low water. While he was there, the water level rose, and it was two days before it dropped and he could sail out.

If the sun is still high and it is too early to consider stopping for the night, there are some spots you could head for down river. At the end of this cruise, about twenty-five miles below Boyer Park, you can anchor at the Port of Garfield or Central Ferry. Along the river there are some inlets to test; just be sure to have adequate water under the keel.

The cluster of silos in the wide curve below Boyer Park stands at Almota, the site of Lewis and Clark's first camp on the lower Snake River. The hills behind Almota lean away from the shore, their rounded slopes reaching to lofty heights. Tugs stop here to pick up barges loaded with grain for delivery on the lower Columbia River.

For the forty years that steamboats plied this same route, picking up freight, passengers, and wheat, there was a "wheat landing" about every three miles. Seldom were the boats delayed: only when the river was too high, too low, or frozen did a shipment wait. Today, some of the small parks along the Snake, such as Illia, Riparia, and Offield, are located near these landings.

The road winds up the hills away from the river at Almota and Illia Landing. Except for the highway from Clarkston to Wawawai along the first part of this cruise, roads do not follow the lower Snake as they do on long stretches of the Columbia. They come from the heights to lead down to a farm or railroad siding, or to cross a dam and touch the river shore just briefly. Trains pass in the early morning or evening, so you rarely see land traffic along the river.

The river expands beyond the curve at Almota. Illia Landing, with a launch ramp, boat dock, grills, picnic tables, and restrooms, occupies a small open area on the south shore.

Wade's Bar, just below the landing, was the site of one of the worst tragedies on the lower Snake. One afternoon in August 1893, with the sun's heat reflecting from the water and hills, a man stood on the sandbar. As the *Annie Faxon* churned down the river from Lewiston on its way to Riparia, the man hailed the steamboat. The *Annie Faxon* turned. As it eased toward the shore, the boiler exploded; crew and passengers were thrown into the water. Some grabbed floating wreckage and were pulled into small boats. Eight people were killed, and many more injured.

Now and then the river swings around large benchlands that look as if a slide fell from the cliffs above. Abandoned farmhouses and remnants of orchards stand on some. Rows of crops score the tops and sides of others. The shorelines fringing these lands offer enticing spots to stop for a swim. There is no need to "toe-test" the water. Just anchor, and plunge in. Warmed by the summer sun, the slow moving water often reaches temperatures of eighty degrees.

If you wade ashore and walk among grass and rocks, watch each step. Here, as in much of the country east of the Cascades, the hot, dry climate is a good habitat for rattlesnakes.

You'll find these shore pockets and inlets located at intervals of about three miles starting three miles below Illia Landing. There is one near Smith Bar and one near Penawawa Canyon. A creek runs down the canyon and forms a narrow bay on the north shore where a railroad bridge (vertical clearance, twelve feet) crosses the entrance. Penawawa, an early wheat landing, was settled in 1870 and little is left today.

Steep cliffs close in on both sides of the river at Penawawa and continue a short distance until they push back along the south shore near Willow Landing. This Corps park, located across from day marker number twenty-one and edged by a sandy beach, forms a wedge between cultivated fields of neighboring farms. One of the farms downstream, its growing patches neatly squared and fenced, is the site of the Central Ferry Research Farm, a joint project of Washington State University and the Agricultural Research Service of the U.S. Department of Agriculture.

As you sail by the farm, the sun now below the hills, tops of silos like shadowy domes appear around the bend at the Port of Central Ferry. This was for a long time a major ferry crossing until the highway bridge was built. After a long day, and with sixty miles between you and Lewiston-Clarkston, you may want to consider securing for the night in the small bay at the Port of Garfield on the south shore, or at Central Ferry State Park across the river.

The bay carved beneath hills is protected from westerly winds, and a launch ramp lies near the silos in the upper end. Should you decide to anchor here for the night, hang the hook near the west side and clear of the loading area in front of the silos, since tugs work the river twenty-four hours a day. At night the captains flip on powerful searchlights as they hook up to or leave a barge. If you are awakened at 2:30 A.M. by the sound of an engine, voices drifting across the water, then a bright light pushing away the darkness as if morning had suddenly dawned, you'll know it's a tug. If you are anchored out of the way, there is no need to leap from bed and move the boat. The tug's wake is minimal—the boat will rock gently, and then all will be quiet and dark again.

Central Ferry State Park spreads across spacious slopes rising slowly from the river. Like a large arena, it presents a contrast to the cliffs and narrow benchlands traveled through earlier on this cruise. Green lawns wander between large parking lots and camping spots with trim wooden windbreaks around picnic tables. Since this is one of the larger parks on the lower Snake, it includes a beach for swimming, a launch ramp, boat dock, and moorage. Winds blow up the canyon, so you may listen the night long to the halyard snap against the mast. But this is a small inconvenience in a secure moorage.

As you settle down for the night you may look down river, but even in this open arena between hills, the river soon bends and disappears. The mystery of what lies around that next bend may pique your curiosity for the next cruise.

# Cruise
# Two

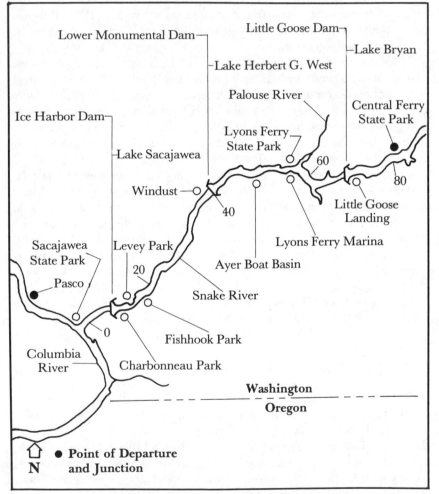

Lower Monumental Dam⌐

Little Goose Dam⌐

⌐Lake Bryan

⌐Lake Herbert G. West

Palouse River

Central Ferry
State Park

Ice Harbor Dam⌐

Lyons Ferry
State Park

⌐Lake Sacajawea

60

Windust ⌐O

80

Little Goose
Landing

40

Sacajawea
State Park

Levey Park

Lyons Ferry Marina

20

Ayer Boat Basin

Pasco

Snake River

0

Fishhook Park

Columbia
River

Charbonneau Park

**Washington**
**Oregon**

⇧   ● **Point of Departure**
**N**   **and Junction**

*Do not use for navigation.*
*Use NOAA Nautical Charts 18547, 18546, and 18545*

# Central Ferry to Tri-Cities

**Point of departure:** Central Ferry State Park
**Course:** Snake River via Lake Bryan and Little Goose Lock and Dam
    with a vertical drop of 98 feet; Lake Herbert G. West and Lower
    Monumental Lock and Dam, with a vertical drop of 100 feet;
    Lake Sacajawea and Ice Harbor Lock and Dam with a vertical
    drop of 100 feet, to the Tri-Cities on the Columbia River
**Stops:** Lyons Ferry Marina, Lyons Ferry State Park, Ayer Boat Basin,
    Windust Park, Fishhook Park, Levey Park, Charbonneau Park,
    Sacajawea Park, Pasco, Kennewick
**Length of cruise:** approximately 80 statute miles
**Duration on power:** 1 to 2 days
**Duration on sail:** 2 to 4 days
**Overnight moorage:** Lyons Ferry Marina, Lyons Ferry State Park,
    Fishhook Park, Charbonneau Park, Pasco, Kennewick
**Junction point for Cruise Three:** Tri-Cities, Washington; Pasco,
    Kennewick, Richland

# Palouse Country

Before we cruised and investigated the lower Snake, we queried one who had been there. "What's it like?" we asked. "Virtually nothing except mule deer," he replied. But we found it otherwise. At night, the sky is filled with stars, stars that are always there but are lost to view over lighted cities. When neither the wind nor a voice nor a motor stirs, the silence is penetrating and hard to believe when you are used to the continual background sounds of radios, cars, and ticking clocks. And, traveling the Palouse country at a leisurely pace, you see gradual changes taking place.

The canyon walls are less steep here than they have been, and wide swales between them now and then reveal fringes of wheat fields, the Palouse country beyond. The origin of the name dates back to the French-Canadian fur trappers. When they crossed the expanse of hills covered by bunch grass, they called it Pelouse country—the grasslands. In the spring, the rolling hilltops bristle with green fields that run for miles beyond the river. When these fields are freshly plowed, the wind sometimes sweeps across the brown furrows, sending clouds of dust into the river's canyons.

Palouse country comes awake slowly and quietly. The river mirrors the crimson tint of morning clouds drifting in silence overhead. A warm breeze laces the wild grasses nearby. These sensations and more greet an early riser before the sun crests above the hills, before a boat skims by on the way to a fishing hole.

Beyond the bend ahead, the river runs deep against steep cliffs to the north. This is the start of Cruise Two, about eighty miles long—longer than the first cruise but with more possibilities for anchoring out. If your timing was such that you did not stop overnight at Central Ferry, several stopping places ahead are marked on the chart. Each is a "gulch," and each is a protected cove on the south shore. New York Gulch is located across from the downstream end of the island sometimes referred to by commercial boaters as "Goose Island." Just below it is Phalen Gulch, and another mile farther down is Dry Gulch.

The next dam, Little Goose Lock and Dam, is about six miles below Dry Gulch. Built in 1970, it was named for an island now covered by water. During the dam construction, archeological excavations uncovered materials that belonged to people who lived in these canyons around 8000 B.C. and hunted elk, bison, deer, and smaller animals.

The lock located on the south side of the dam has a drop of 98 feet, and it takes thirty to forty minutes for the locking-through process. Should you have a long wait before entering the lock, you can tie up at Little Goose Landing a mile upstream. When you emerge downstream, move straight out beyond the wing wall to avoid the faster moving current in front of the spillway. Also, here at Little Goose, watch for winds that may be blowing up the canyon causing the boat to be "headed," or pushed back, as you maneuver away from the dam.

The lake you are now cruising is Lake Herbert G. West, the pool behind Lower Monumental Lock and Dam. It is twenty-nine miles long, and is considered by some the best fishing lake on the lower Snake. Fishermen catch smallmouth bass, steelhead, and channel cats. One cat caught recently weighed twenty-three pounds.

In 1980 the Corps of Engineers worked to restore wildlife habitats lost when waters rose behind the dams on the Snake. The restored areas were developed to mitigate the loss of 120,000 man-days of hunting per year. The selected areas were fenced and farmed to produce feed and forage for the area's game, and hunting is now allowed in the cultivated areas. The areas where work was done are scattered along the river; one is just below Little Goose on the south shore.

In front of Riparia, which was once a "wheat landing," old railroad stone bridge abutments stand slightly above the water on both shores. The stone was quarried from Granite Point and set as piers in 1881.

Before the river was tamed to slack water, it started a swift descent near the present Texas Rapids Corps Park and continued almost to the mouth of the Tucannon River four miles downstream. The park, below Riparia, is located near the head of these old rapids.

Lewis and Clark saw the rapids on a day when they had traveled only thirty miles. Since they wanted to investigate the rapids before running them, they camped for the night. The next day, they found them "very dangerous about two miles in length and strewed with rocks in every direction, so as to require great dexterity to avoid running against them." Two miles below these rapids, they ran another one and then passed the mouth of the Tucannon River, the largest tributary flowing into the lower Snake River from the south. Today a nagivation marker is hung on the large rock abutment where the two rivers merge.

First an army fort and then a town stood near the mouth of the Tucannon. Fort Taylor was built during war with the Indians, but the army used it from only August to October 1858. Fifteen years later, farmers formed the Grange Warehouse Company, started a freight and shipping point, and Grange City had its beginning. But when a rail line was completed several miles south of the town in 1881, the population dwindled. Yet in 1941, Grange City was still on the map with a population of two.

The river continues a narrow course between craggy basalt bluffs as it flows under a railroad bridge (vertical clearance, fifty-two feet), past grain silos to the mouth of the Palouse River on the north and Turner Bay on the south. Overhead, a highway bridge and the nation's highest working trestle span the Snake.

Here in a setting rimmed by sculptured cliffs you will find a marina, a park, a river to kayak, history to explore, and trails to hike. Tucked in Turner Bay on the south shore below the highway bridge, Lyons Ferry Marina, open year-round, has moorage, gas, groceries, ice, showers, and a lift. Boating club members who trailer their boats or come up river from the Tri-Cities or Portland, use the marina as headquarters. During the day they soak up the sun at Lyons Ferry State Park across the Snake River. This beautifully landscaped park covers a knoll where the Palouse River merges with the Snake. At bulkheaded tie-ups you can wrap the line around a cleat and step out onto the grass.

Take a short stroll through the park along the Palouse and you'll find an old ferry boat moored quietly behind tall rushes. This ferry, like the ferries that crossed the Snake here for over one hundred years, was hooked to an overhead cable strung across the river. Lee boards fore and aft were dropped or lifted depending on the direction of the crossing. The push of the current against the downed lee board powered the ferry. The ferry is now in the registry for State Historic Artifacts. N.A. Turner and his wife, Ruth, ran the ferry for twenty-three years; Turner guided its last crossing in December 1968.

A short run up the Palouse River brings you to the Marmes Rock Shelter, an Indian burial site dating back to 8000 B.C. Excavations here before Lower Monumental Dam was completed yielded some of the oldest human fossils found in the Western Hemisphere. Beyond the Rock Shelter, the river quickly narrows and is navigable for deep draft boats just a short distance. Kayakers, however, portage their slim boats to just below Palouse Falls, where the river plunges over cliffs 190 feet high. From here they ride the river down through a narrow, dark canyon colored by bunch grass and wildflowers.

Concern that another Indian burial site—this one of more recent origin—would be inundated by the lake's waters led to the excavation of the Palouse Indian Cemetery. During the digging, a silver Lewis and Clark peace medal was found. As the two explorers traveled across the West, they awarded forty silver medals to prominent Indian chiefs. Six have been found. The one uncovered in the Palouse Cemetery is now with the Nez Perce Indians.

Before leaving Lyons Ferry, check your gas gauge and water supply. The next place to buy gas is nearly fifty miles downstream at Charbonneau Park.

You may leave Lyons Ferry with some regret, but once you are on your way there is no chance for lingering looks back. Just as quickly as you came upon it, it disappears behind you. As you nose the boat down river, you swing below Steamboat Bend and Lyons Ferry is out of sight.

Although forty miles separate you from the next park with moorage, you will find more inlets and coves notched into the shoreline where you can anchor. Many appear on the chart and will help in your planning for a lunch or an overnight stop. There is a good one on the north shore across from Ayer about six miles away. As you approach this Union Pacific crew station, look for a line of boxcars strung out east of the community. White houses trimmed in green and a vacant school stand above the river. Thirty years ago, thirty-five railroad families lived here. Visitors to Ayer could stop at a hotel and buy dinner in the restaurant. The old hotel, weathered, its windows gone, still sits in a field on a hillside above the town, its amenities no longer required in the age of diesel locomotives.

The Ayer Boat Basin, with a ramp, dock, picnic tables, and restrooms, is down river on the south shore, behind a fill for railroad tracks, near marker number nineteen. Should you want to proceed inside, look for a rock jetty that extends out from a culvert opening under the tracks. Clearance is twelve feet.

Several species of wildlife may be observed along this isolated stretch of river. During migration, geese and wild ducks that use this lake as a seasonal flyway are seen and heard flapping overhead in scattered Vs. Sitting quietly on the stern while waiting for nightfall, you may catch sight of a badger, deer, or bobcat, or hear the distant howl of a coyote.

A large outcropping of basalt stands in a wide curve on the river a few miles before you reach Lower Monumental Lock and Dam. It looms high above the sloping land around it. This is Monumental Rock, which gives its name to the dam.

The lock and dam are set in a Snake River gorge that is two hundred feet deep. As you move closer to the lock, the two towers, one on either side of the gate, look like massive turrets from a medieval castle. The hills beyond mound up high against a blue sky. This dam, like others along the inland waterway, has a room for viewing fish swimming up the ladder. Depending on the time of year, visitors can watch spring, summer, and fall Chinook and steelhead as they push their way upstream. Lower Monumental Lock began operation in 1969, and later that same year two power generating units started up.

If you left Lyons Ferry in the morning, you may be looking for a shady place to stop for lunch. As you have noticed, shade trees on the lower Snake are a rarity, so the wooded park you will come to three miles below the lock stands out as an oasis. This is Windust Park and Port, named not for the local weather but for a man who once ran the ferry here.

There are picnic tables and grills, a swimming beach, launch ramp, and small boat dock. Geese sometimes waddle about in the park, grabbing tidbits in the grass, and pigeons flock around the silos at the port, where they find the spilled grain easy pickings.

A tall, rectangular grain elevator stands on a slope behind the park. It is an example of an earlier style, built with two by twelve planks laid one on top of the other. This method of construction made such elevators almost indestructible, so you will see more of these as you move down river.

Once you are settled under the spreading trees at Windust Park, you may find it difficult to pack up and leave. If your preference is for stopping at parks, don't pass this one up, for when you check the chart you will see that the next one is twenty miles down river, or about two-thirds of the way on Lake Sacajawea, the lake you are now on. This stretch is the longest without a park or a corps landing. There are few roads, and those that do dip down to the river are usually dirt or gravel. The names of the places where they stop appear on the chart: Scott, Snake River Junction, Sheffler. For a boater who is on the river for the first time and is unfamiliar with the territory, these names may signify a small community or a place with a store. Thinking, "Ahh, a place to get a cold beer," he is disappointed to find a grain elevator instead.

Lake Sacajawea lies behind Ice Harbor Lock and Dam, the last step on the lower Snake River. Eight miles below the dam the Snake merges with the Columbia. The waters of the lake move slowly, taking a week to pass from Lower Monumental to Ice Harbor. They meander through short canyons and by broad bottomlands. In the distance, hills slant away; some of their edges are carved in high, banked cliffs.

For awhile, the railroads seem a part of the landscape—not for their noise but for their structures. Webbed trestles of the Burlington Northern high on the north side cross several canyons. Below the trestle at Burr Canyon, a few miles past Windust, a large cave opens onto the river shore.

On cliffs through this area, like those across from Snake River Junction, petroglyphs drawn by early Indians have been found. Around the bend below Snake River Junction to Anchor Canyon, a distance of about five miles, there are several good places to drop the

*Indian Memorial, original petroglyphs, at Ice Harbor Lock and Dam*

hook. A large cove on the south side just before Anchor Canyon is well protected from westerlies. When we came by here early one Sunday morning, two boats were moored and rocking peacefully. Hills rise to the south. Once covered with grass, the hills are now planted with rows of fruit trees. To the west are the short cliffs of Anchor Canyon. The canyon is a narrow chute a little over a mile long, and the narrowest place on the lower Snake. Along the shores, here and downstream, you will see metal pans on stands. These are goose-nesting sites built by the corps to mitigate the loss of natural sites.

Boating traffic picks up after Anchor Canyon. Water-skiers cut trails across the river, and small runabouts are pulled up on the beaches. Some vacationers have launched their boats at Fishhook Park (just ahead and about seven miles above Ice Harbor), others at Levey and Charbonneau parks, and still others have locked-through the dam. Being close to Kennewick, Pasco, and Richland, the three parks are popular summer gathering places. All have launch ramps and docks. Levey Park, the only one on the north shore, also has deep moorage.

At Charbonneau you will find Ice Harbor Marina. They have overnight moorage for a fee, gas and diesel, and a place to shower.

The river above Levey and down to Charbonneau is wide, and gusty winds often blow in the afternoon. The Sunday races held here by sailing clubs are quite a sight, with sailors jockeying for position to find the best wind as a tug moves downstream pushing barges, and power-boats loaded with people zip by to a swimming beach.

Ice Harbor Lock and Dam were named for a small cove now covered by water just upstream from the dam. Sternwheelers carrying men anxious to arrive at the Idaho goldfields took shelter in the cove while they waited for the spring breakup of ice on the river. The dam began generating power in 1961, and the lock was opened for commercial traffic in 1962.

Locking-through Ice Harbor on a weekend may seem like trying to get through an intersection at rush hour. Boaters come up from the Columbia to spend a few hours on Lake Sacajawea, or to take a ride in the lock. While waiting to enter the lock to go downstream, we once watched fifteen pleasure boats pour out of the lock in front of a tug and barge like children bursting out of school when the last bell rings.

When you are outside and waiting for a tug or pleasure boat to clear the lock, stay out of the way. Some skippers who are anxious to get in but are not sure what to do cause problems by dodging around the exiting vessels. There is plenty of time to enter and secure before the gates close. You can lock-through with a tug and barge, if there is room and they are not carrying hazardous cargo. This is true for all locks. Once the lock-tender gives you the "go-ahead," let the tug proceed first and secure before you move in. If the floating mooring bitts are taken and you cannot find someone to raft to, you can tie to a cleat on the barge.

*Ice Harbor Lock and Dam*

Once you have secured inside and before the gates close, turn and take one last look up the miles of hills and canyons that you have come through. You may say, as we always do, "We'll be back."

When you emerge from the lock you will have only a short run to the Columbia, but this is not the time to relax navigational skills. For one thing, the current may be swift. Its speed varies with the amount of water in Lake Wallula, the lake you are now on, and the amount being released over the spillway. Sometimes there is no release. One day when we came through, Lake Wallula was six feet higher at the base of Ice Harbor than at the Columbia River, and the current was running eight knots.

Although the river is wide below the dam, the channel is narrow. Stay between the buoy markers and the north shore. In late summer, some of the riverbed to the south of the markers is dry. The channel, well marked, stays near the north shore for about four miles through high banks. The McNary National Wildlife Refuge borders the south bank. It is one of many preserves along the Pacific Flyway and is an important feeding and resting place for migrating waterfowl. Ahead, the tops of bridges and tank farms at the Tri-Cities protrude above the fields and trees.

The channel angles south on the east end of Strawberry Island. Hood Park, used mostly by picnickers, water-skiers, and campers, is on the south shore above the highway bridge. There is a launch ramp, a small handling dock, ski dock, and showers.

The last bridge on the Snake is the Northern Pacific Railroad Bridge near the confluence with the Columbia. The bridge has a vertical clearance of fourteen feet when the lift span is down.

Sacajawea Park spreads northeast between the Snake and Columbia. This large park was built in the 1920s on an Indian midden, or refuse heap. A launch ramp and dock are inside a small cove that is entered from the Snake. The Sacajawea Interpretive Center, which is part of the park, is one of three such centers in Washington on the Lewis and Clark Trail. One wing at the center interprets Sacajawea's role with the expedition, and the other wing contains a collection of Indian artifacts from the Columbia and Snake river areas.

A swing to the northwest around the park will take your boat onto the Columbia in the direction of the Tri-Cities, junction point for the next cruise.

# Cruise
# Three

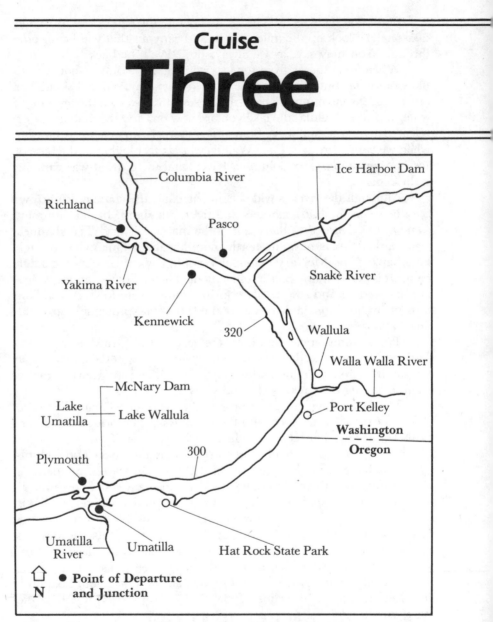

Columbia River

Ice Harbor Dam

Richland

Pasco

Yakima River

Snake River

Kennewick

320

Wallula

Walla Walla River

McNary Dam

Lake Umatilla

Lake Wallula

Port Kelley

**Washington**
**Oregon**

Plymouth

300

Umatilla River

Umatilla

Hat Rock State Park

⌂ ● **Point of Departure**
**N** **and Junction**

*Do not use for navigation.*
*Use NOAA Nautical Charts 18542 and 18541*

# Tri-Cities to Plymouth and Umatilla

**Point of departure:** Tri-Cities, Washington; Pasco, Kennewick, Richland

**Course:** Columbia River via Lake Wallula and McNary Lock and Dam, with a vertical drop of 75 feet to Lake Umatilla

**Stops:** Walla Walla Yacht Club, McNary Yacht Club, Hat Rock State Park, Plymouth Park, Umatilla Marina

**Length of cruise:** approximately 40 statute miles

**Duration on power:** 1 day

**Duration on sail:** 2 days

**Overnight moorage:** Plymouth Park, Umatilla Marina

**Junction point for Cruise Four:** Umatilla, Oregon; Plymouth, Washington

# Tri-Cities and Wallula Gap

When the boat's keel first cleaves the waters of the Columbia River, you have traveled about one-third of the distance down the inland waterway and are now on the main artery of the Pacific Northwest. Some refer to this point as the beginning of the typical cruise—Pasco to Astoria. These three words describe only a portion of the route, and conjure up few images of the contrasts and varieties to be seen and experienced as you travel the next 325 miles to the bar.

Cruise Three, though one of the shorter cruises, is a study in contrasts as part of it follows a course through two corridorlike stretches on Lake Wallula, the pool behind McNary Lock and Dam.

The first corridor passes through the Tri-Cities, upstream on the Columbia from its confluence with the Snake. Its sides are decorated with parks, tank farms, and motels; its skyline is spanned by four bridges. Here, nearly 100,000 people live in one of the largest metropolitan areas in Washington east of the Cascades.

The second corridor is Wallula Gap, about fifteen miles downstream. Where it passes through Horse Heaven Hills, its sides are brown basalt cliffs. The monochrome brown is relieved by the greens, reds, and bronzes of lichen, and by the yellows and purples of wildflowers in the spring.

Since the filling of Lake Wallula in 1953, the Tri-Cities—Kennewick, Pasco, and Richland—have become headquarters for recreational boating in this region. Sunshine 280 days a year, hot summer days, broad waters for skiing, swimming, and inner-tubing have drawn many to this lake. For weekends or week-long vacations, people come to camp in shaded parks and launch their boats onto the lake. There are pleasure boats aplenty here, and you will notice that almost all are trailerable. The many ramps dotting the rivers' shores are a reflection of this.

Although the theoretical head of navigation on the Columbia River is Priest Rapids Dam, about forty-five miles above the Tri-Cities, the practical one is at the last navigation marker in front of the Rivershore Dunes Motel in Richland. The river above this point is uncharted, and its waters shallow and filled with shoals. However, boaters with local knowledge do use the river above Richland. An unofficial chart is published locally and is available at Metz Marine Store in Kennewick. It is not intended for navigation, but it does give a good idea of upstream waters.

As these three cities grew—their boundaries reached out, touched, and eventually became linked by bridges—they were lumped together and referred to as one. Yet each has its own interesting history.

Kennewick has its roots in Indian history. The name is derived from an Indian word meaning "winter heaven." Winter temperatures were mild. In the nearby hills, now called Horse Heaven Hills, the Indians left their horses to graze belly deep in bunch grass, while they fished for salmon in the Yakima River. In October of 1805, Clark and two men explored a short distance up the Columbia near the mouth of the Yakima and shared a meal of boiled salmon with the Indians. Clark later wrote that the Columbia here was "... so clear that the salmon may be seen swimming in the water at the depth of 15 to 20 feet."

About sixty years later the first settlement appeared at the mouth of the Yakima River. After several name changes the small community took the name Kennewick in 1883.

A year later, across the Columbia, Pasco was platted by the Northern Pacific Railroad. Soon a ferry carrying trains ran between the two communities.

Several versions for the origin of the name, Pasco, have been told, but the most reliable gives credit to Virgil Bogue, a railroad surveyor for Northern Pacific. Prior to working for Northern Pacific, Bogue worked in the South American Andes near a mining camp named Cerro de Pasco, a windy and dusty place. During Bogue's first day along the Columbia, a dust storm blew reminding him of the mining camp, and he named the new community Pasco.

Richland's history mirrors the growth of a "gold rush" town. Before World War II, it was a small farming hamlet. Then, in 1943, the original site of Hanford Works was built north of town. Construction and management workers moved in and the population boomed. Hanford Works is now engaged in nuclear research for energy, production of materials, and disposal of nuclear waste.

As you move up the Columbia toward the Tri-Cities, you will find Water World Marina in Pasco located just east of the railroad bridge. Open year-round, they have gas and water and can provide general boat repairs.

Beyond the railroad bridge (vertical clearance eighteen feet) with a lift opening arc two highway bridges, one old, one new, which span the river side by side. Each has a forty-nine foot clearance. The old one, built in 1920, replaced the ferry crossing between Pasco and Kennewick. It was scheduled for demolition when the new bridge was completed in 1978. But since then, it has been the focus of a dispute between those who want to preserve it and those who want to tear it down.

The new bridge is the only stayed cable bridge in North America. Considered a distinguished engineering feat, its cables radiate like spokes from the towers and hold the roadway in compression to create a rigid system. It is highly visible up and down the river, and on an early summer evening, its gleaming cables appear like a celestial harp.

Just beyond the bridge in Kennewick is Clover Island. Built of river dredgings, it is the home of two great restaurants, the U.S. Coast Guard Station, and Metz Marina. This marina provides a number of boaters' needs, including gas, water, boat ramp, lift and repairs, and showers. They also have transient moorage. With your boat moored at Metz you can call for a taxi or catch a ride to the nearest shopping center to stock up on supplies. But if your first priority is eating, try the nationally known Cedars Restaurant, or the panoramic view from the Captain's Table atop the Clover Island Motel. If you need to wash up, you might consider the motel for an overnight stay.

The Port of Kennewick, also on Clover Island, has a ramp, restrooms, and showers. Upstream in Richland you will find Columbia Park Marina where you can get water, gas, and engine repairs.

There are several recreation areas along the shores of the cities' corridor. Columbia Park, a well-appointed park with picnic areas, boat ramps and docks, and campground, stretches along the river above Clover Island toward Richland. Only a thin line of beach separates its long, wide green lawns from the blue waters of the river. Other parks, all with launch ramps and spots to enjoy a lunch or supper, include: Leslie R. Groves Park above Richland, Howard Amon Park in Richland, Chiawana Park on the east side of the river across from the mouth of the Yakima River, and Riverhaven above Pasco. Any one of these parks provides access to good fishing for crappie and perch. Some say this is the best bass fishing around.

Not all the appeal is limited to the river. If you have shore time, or if this will be your only visit to the Tri-Cities, we recommend a layover with time spent touring. The Hanford Science Center in downtown Richland features exhibits of energy sources, and the visitor center at the Fast Flux Test Facility on the northern edge of Richland has a fascinating display and models of the "fast breeder" reactor.

As you leave the Tri-Cities your course will begin curving in a long arch. The Columbia flows southeasterly past the confluence with the Snake, then begins gradually to swing westward past Horse Heaven Hills and through Wallula Gap.

Below the Snake, and beyond a railroad lift bridge (clearance eleven feet), the river is broad, the shoreline sparsely settled. The miles of open river ahead give the feeling of sailing on an inland lake. To the south, the lofty, bare mountains rise at what appears to be the lake's

*Columbia Park*

end. To the west, the low slopes rise quickly to Horse Heaven Hills. To the east, rolling plains run for mile after mile to Walla Walla and beyond to the Blue Mountain range, still snow-covered in spring.

The "drift" of this area collecting around bridge abutments and floating across the water tells of the dry climate: it is sagebrush. Sometimes the river seems almost choked with the skeletal brown balls of sage torn from the dry soil and blown onto the water.

Because of the open aspect of this stretch, the winds that blow here can wreak havoc with the lake's surface. These waters are changeable and unpredictable. On one of our trips, the water was a mirror reflecting the distant progress of a toylike train running alongside the hills. On another, we cooled ourselves in the late summer afternoon by sitting on the bow and letting the spray from the slightly choppy waters fly against us. At times like these, there are no hints of other possibilities. Yet, we have seen this stretch so rough that the waters torn by the pull of winds whirled into waterspouts. When the winds rise, the best advice is to get off the open water quickly.

Foundation Island, just a few miles downstream from the railroad bridge, is a good anchorage for a lunch stop for deep draft boats. Farther downstream a large bar juts out from the eastern shore into the lake near Homly Channel. The waters and bar look inviting, but resist the temptation, as it is accessible only by rowboat or canoe. Southeast of the bar, steam plumes rise from stacks at a Boise Cascade pulp mill. Just down river is the town of Wallula near the mouth of the Walla Walla River. The lake derives its name from this historic town. Wallula is an Indian term meaning "many waters." Now much of the original town is submerged.

Located near the site of the Hudson's Bay Company's Fort Walla Walla, Wallula is the second oldest town in Washington. Walla Walla is the oldest, and boaters may be more familiar with it. This town, thirty miles up the Walla Walla River, was the home of the Whitman Mission. Established in 1836 by Dr. Marcus Whitman, the mission became an important stop on the Oregon Trail. In 1847 the mission was attacked by Indians. Dr. Whitman and his wife, Narcissa, and twelve others were killed in what is now known as the Whitman Massacre.

Walla Walla became an agricultural center, and in 1875 it was linked to Wallula by the "Rawhide Railroad." This short, narrow-gauge line ran between Walla Walla and Wallula, which was the nearest port for wheat growing country. The railroad was the ingenious idea of Dr. Dorsey Baker, a physician with a Moses-like beard. He built it in response to farmers' complaints about the high rates charged for horse-drawn wagons to haul their grain. Confronted with the high price of iron rails, Dr. Baker built wooden rails with strips of iron on top and later wrapped with rawhide—so one story goes—and hence, the name "Rawhide Railroad." Officially known as the Walla Walla and Columbia River Railroad, it cut the cost of overland freight rates for wheat farmers and led to the planting of many more acres. The line was later purchased by the Oregon Navigation and Steamship Company, and eventually by Union Pacific.

When the rivers ran free, the Snake and Columbia still retained their identities at Wallula. The currents of the Columbia were cold, and held to mid-channel and the western shore. Those of the Snake were warmer and flowed along the eastern shore. A traveler in the mid-1800s noted this: he wrote that Indians desiring a cold drink on a hot day paddled to mid-channel to scoop up waters of the Columbia.

Below Wallula the Columbia finally commences its turn to the west and cuts through Horse Heaven Hills, creating Wallula Gap. This corridor extends several miles west to a point near Hat Rock, about six miles above McNary Lock and Dam.

A prominent landmark stands above the river to port. The

double-crowned butte called "Two Sisters" on the chart has also been called "Twin Captains" and "Two Virgins." In the bight below is Port Kelley, marked by a large grain elevator. Adjacent to the grain-loading facility is the Walla Walla Yacht Club. Facilities are limited, but this club honors other yacht club members and will help non-members. Its location provides a good wind haven.

Although there are no white lines across the river or up the sides of the cliffs to mark the boundary, you cross into Oregon about two miles downstream. A red flashing light, "Bull Run" or "14" on the chart, is near the state line. From this point to the Pacific Ocean, the river serves as the boundary between Washington and Oregon.

Through stretches like this, with few distinguishing landmarks to help boaters determine their location quickly, there is a way you can keep track of where you are. When a road skirts the river, as it does here on the Oregon side, pull out the binoculars and read the mileage signs to the next town. The road is not always so helpful, however: if you are running at night and watching for lighted buoys, the headlights of moving cars can be confusing.

If you enjoy desert wildflowers, spring is the time to boat these waters. Masses of yellow couse and goldstar bloom first. Before their colors fade, clusters of pink phlox, blue lupine, orange mallow, and wild sunflowers can be seen growing among the sage and prickly pear cactus. During summer sailboat races, the Gap blossoms with brightly colored spinnakers.

Gradually the hills push back, and you sail from the basalt corridor past Juniper Canyon in Oregon, marked by a scattering of its namesake trees.

Lewis and Clark saw the next landmark, Hat Rock, in 1805, but mentioned it only in passing. At the time, their attention was focused on negotiating rapids. Lewis described "a rock on the left shore which is 14 miles from our camp of last night and resembles a hat in shape."

Hat Rock stands back from the river near two popular boating and camping areas, McNary Yacht Club and Hat Rock State Park. Facilities at this private yacht club are for members' use. Yet, in the case of an emergency or high winds, other boaters are welcome. Just upstream from the yacht club there is a protected cove for anchoring, but watch the depths and remember that the lake waters can be drawn down.

Private homes dot the point between the club and Hat Rock State Park to the west. Although the park has no overnight facilities for boaters, a cove in from the river offers a small craft haven during high winds. Grass and trees cover the park grounds and surround a small lake. In addition to a boat ramp, there are picnic areas, hiking trails, and a swimming beach.

*Hat Rock State Park*

When you are about a half-hour out from the McNary Locks, call ahead and let them know you are coming. It takes about thirty minutes to lock-through and drop the seventy-five feet while thirty-eight million gallons of water are being released.

Named for the late Senator Charles McNary of Oregon, the dam is the first as you descend the Columbia, and is 292 miles from the ocean. It was the first post-World War II multipurpose dam constructed on the Columbia River. At the time, those opposed to its construction questioned the benefits of a dam in sagebrush and jackrabbit country.

As you move out from the locks, be on the lookout for fishermen. This is a popular fishing spot, and usually abounds with small fishing craft. This, combined with a strong current, makes maneuvering tricky. You are now on Lake Umatilla. Umatilla is an old Indian word used to name the river downstream on the Oregon shore.

Below the highway bridge just down from the dam there are two possible overnight moorages. One is at Plymouth, Washington. Plymouth Park, on an island in front of the town and connected to the mainland by a bridge, has overnight camping and trailer hookups. There is also a launch ramp and moorage, but no gas.

Those wanting more facilities should head into Umatilla Marina. This marina, open year-round, offers gas, diesel, and overnight moorage. The harbor is not close to downtown, but the marina operator will provide or find rides for boaters who need to get to town for supplies.

Umatilla started out as a landing for river traffic and goods going to the Idaho goldfields in the early 1860s. One man owned the land, but in the boomtown atmosphere no one paid attention to his right of ownership. Despite his protests a hundred buildings still stood on his land.

If you visit Umatilla during the late summer and early fall, you are right in time for watermelon season. Take the time to buy a plump, ripe melon, and after dinner, pass out big hunks to the crew.

*McNary Dam*

# Cruise
# Four

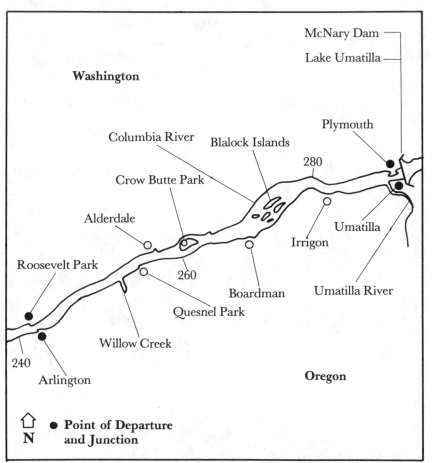

McNary Dam
Lake Umatilla

Washington

Columbia River     Blalock Islands
Crow Butte Park                          280
                                              Plymouth
Alderdale
Roosevelt Park                            Umatilla
                              260          Irrigon
                    Quesnel Park     Boardman     Umatilla River
             Willow Creek
240
   Arlington                                      Oregon

N     ● Point of Departure
         and Junction

*Do not use for navigation.*
*Use NOAA Nautical Charts 18539, 18537, and 18536*

# Plymouth and Umatilla to Roosevelt and Arlington

**Point of departure:** Umatilla, Oregon; or Plymouth, Washington
**Course:** Columbia River via Lake Umatilla
**Stops:** Irrigon, Boardman Park, Crow Butte Park, Quesnel Park, Roosevelt Park, Arlington
**Length of cruise:** approximately 50 statute miles
**Duration on power:** 1 day
**Duration on sail:** 2 to 3 days
**Overnight moorage:** Crow Butte Park, Roosevelt Park, Arlington
**Junction point for Cruise Five:** Roosevelt Park, Washington; Arlington, Oregon

# Desert and Irrigated Fields

On a still morning an orange glow rims the eastern horizon. Lake Umatilla, the pool behind John Day Dam, is flat as a millpond while hummocks covered with desert sage and grasses roll away from its shores. The endless expanse of water, sky, and land gives you the feeling of being moored somewhere in the southwestern plains. Travelers by car may feel it is a dull, monotonous passage. But in the midst of such a quiet landscape you, as a boater, will find your perceptions sharpened. You'll see and enjoy features missed by those hurrying by in a car or train.

As the morning sun moves higher, and its heat fills the cockpit and cabin, you may be anxious to leave the moorage to catch whatever breeze there is on the river. Later in the day, the breeze can whip into wind. There is a prevailing westerly wind in this region, and from March through July, dust storms may blow. Should you be sailing or motoring here then, watch the sky as well as the water. At the first sign of a brown cloud approaching over the desert, move off the open water, for in fifteen to twenty minutes dust and winds of thirty to fifty miles an hour will blow across the river.

Along this forty-seven-mile stretch the parks and marinas—including Irrigon, Boardman, Crow Butte, Roosevelt, and Arlington—offer a haven from the wind and hot sun. Many of these once were ferry landings, none of them large.

Unlike the deep waters extending from shore to shore through Wallula Gap, the waters of Lake Umatilla are shallow, with frequent shoaling outside the channel. Because the channel, which has a minimum depth of nineteen feet, winds through the broad waters of the lake, follow the charts and markers carefully.

When the dry hummocks and flats beyond are irrigated, they support fields of alfalfa and grain crops. From the river you may see crescents of green or hear the giant sprinklers sput-sputting as they turn and throw out water pumped from the river. The first town down river derives its name from this process: Irrigon is a contraction of the words "irrigation" and "Oregon."

The boat basin at Irrigon is the toy harbor of the river, a miniaturized reflection of the traditional jetty, entrance, and floats. It is tempting to call it "cute," but that is hardly an acceptable boater's term. Facilities include a paved boat ramp, restrooms, and a picnic and swimming area. These are for day use only. If you need groceries, you'll have to take a five-block walk to a small shopping area located alongside a two-lane highway.

The site of the original town of Irrigon, established in 1863, now lies beneath the lake's waters. It was a wild and rowdy transfer point for equipment bound for the gold mines in Idaho Territory. The population dropped when gold mining ceased, but nearly a century later it surged again when McNary Dam was built.

Just down river before a broad bend, an old white schoolhouse, now a private residence, stands out on the Washington side. Nearby is a ramp of sorts that is usable at low water. Small boats can be pulled ashore, where a few trees offer shade. This is part of the Umatilla National Wildlife Refuge, which covers more than 22,000 acres of marsh, water, and land on both sides of the river. Waterfowl, including Canada geese, winter and nest here. Chukar, quail, and pheasants feed in the croplands. Fish and small animals also find homes in the refuge.

It is eerie to travel these waters in small boats, as many hunters and fishermen do. Looking down, they see and move over the tops of telephone poles marching along this section of flooded land. During low water, bits of an old highway rise into view. The backwaters of the John Day Dam engulfed this land in 1968 while vestiges of its settlement were still intact.

Beyond the bend the river turns in a more westerly direction, and the main channel flows along the south shore past a collection of sparsely covered low reefs called Blalock Islands. They look uninteresting, and seem to be a place where not much has happened. Here, too, the rising waters of Lake Umatilla slipped across the lower levels and left the higher ones dry, thus changing the once singular Blalock Island—then two miles long—to the present-day plural. The island was named for Nelson Blalock, a surgeon in the Civil War and one of the best-known pioneers in Walla Walla County, Washington. Pursuing his ambition to extend and improve fruit culture, he planted and operated a fruit orchard on the island.

Before Blalock planted his orchards, the Umatilla Indians used the island as a stronghold against horse raids by Snake Indians. The Indians also used the island as a place to dispose of their dead. When Lewis and Clark stopped here in 1805 on their descent of the river, they found a large Indian burial vault. The vault, located on the upstream side of the island, measured sixty by twenty-one feet. It was made of boards and pieces of canoes leaning against a ridgepole. Inside, they found human bones, fishing nets, wooden bowls, skin robes, and trinkets. Vault burial was common among the Indians of the Snake and

*The Columbia River near Boardman, Oregon*

Columbia rivers. Memaloose, from the Chinook jargon for dead, is a name given to several islands down river that were the sites of vault burials.

With the sun high and winds and water calm, the skiers or swimmers on board may be unlashing skis or digging in the duffle bag for swimsuits. Boardman Park at Boardman, Oregon, or Crow Butte Park, about six miles farther down river on the Washington side, are good places to stop for either sport. Both parks charge a fee for their extensive amenities.

Sandy shores spread along the river in front of Boardman. The stubby metal cylinders that look like androids standing in silent packs are in reality pumping stations for irrigation systems. In the waters around Boardman, watch the depth sounder and stay in the marked channel. "Sand moles," or dredges, move in and out trailing sand. The small craft basin is protected by a stone breakwater, with moorage and a launch ramp inside. This large park also has overnight camping, as well as an enclosed swim area with a diving platform—ideal for children. If you missed the watermelons at Umatilla, you can take a short walk into town to pick some up here at a roadside stand.

The river above and below Boardman is two to three miles wide and seems extremely broad compared with other reaches of the inland waterway. The main channel follows the Oregon shore in a southwesterly direction to the Port of Boardman, then turns west toward Crow Butte Island, a long, sage-covered hill. West of Crow

Butte, hills fold and lift on the Washington side as they begin forming the eastern edge of the Cascade Mountains. South of the river, the lowlands still prevail.

Enter Crow Butte Park from the downriver side of the island. An approach from the north is not possible due to shoaling and a causeway that connects the island with the mainland. On a hot summer day, seeing the open, green lawns of the park, you will feel as if a cool glass of water has just been spilled over you. There are no supplies or gas pumps here, but there are many recreational facilities.

Boaters can lauch their boats at either of two ramps, or drop the hook in the moorage, safe from winds that may suddenly romp up the river. Picnic spots dot the lawns, as do young willows. Camping trailers can hook-up for overnight stays. Children can wade or swim along the beach, or tramp beyond the park up the hillside. Here, as in other places east of the Cascades, watch for rattlesnakes. When you walk through the sage, look before you step. When you climb a rock, look before you take a handhold.

On both sides of the river, highways—the interstate in Oregon and the state highway in Washington—and the tracks of the Union Pacific and Burlington Northern railroads all move closer to the river to follow the drainage through the Cascades. From here, with few exceptions, the highways and railroads continue along the Columbia River almost to the ocean, 260 miles away.

Some nights, along this or other stretches of the river, you will hear a sound above the wind as a transcontinental freight coils along the embankment above. Apparently connected with the river only by its path, its course and history are in fact deeply tied to the river. The caboose's fading clatter could be the rattle of a steamboat's bones.

Early transportation along the river was hampered by the long series of rapids between Celilo Falls and The Dalles and the shorter rapids at the Cascades. Before 1860, the river's transportation network was a combination of competing steamboat lines, linked loosely by feuding portage operators with horse-drawn railcars and wagons. Whoever could control the portages around these downstream barriers could control the course of the waterway's empire.

Enter Captain John C. Ainsworth. Ainsworth had been a Mississippi River pilot, and had the instincts of a riverboat gambler. With backing from Portland financiers, he consolidated the interests of competing portages at the Cascades, a wagon road around Celilo Falls, and the steamboats then in service from Portland to Lewiston. Under the name of the Oregon Steam Navigation Company (OSN), the new firm began operating just as gold was being discovered in Idaho. In less than a year, the OSN earned forty-eight percent on its investment.

By 1868, the OSN house flag flew over nearly two dozen steamboats, portage railroads serviced by steam locomotives, and several palatial hotels. The OSN was king of transportation on the river. That same year, Ainsworth watched Northern Pacific railroad surveyors working down river in search of a route to link the east and the Pacific Northwest by rail. Ainsworth saw the threat that rail could bring to his prosperous steamboat empire. Using his established portage railroads and their rights of way as leverage, and watching his timing closely, he sold the OSN interests to the Northern Pacific, thus ensuring that the first principal transcontinental rail link would follow the Columbia's south shore to Portland. This line was not completed until 1882, but after that, feeder lines proliferated throughout the inland empire. The preeminence of the steamboats faded, but their roots are to be found in the rails that replaced them.

Now you hear the muted sounds of trucks and cars. Many zip by on the interstate, but only a few are on the Washington highway. Place names on the chart are scattered, and large cities are many miles away. Whether fighting the winds or relaxing as the keel slices through the water speckled by the sun, you may feel quite alone. At Maryhill (down river) and Paterson (near Crow Butte), Washington officials have marked this stretch with signs that read "No service for 66 miles."

The river in front of Alderdale, Washington, near Alder Creek, is wide, and the current at times seems almost to have stopped. The creek flows from a mountainous amphitheater, covered in summer with the purples and yellows of wildflowers. The current was relatively slow here even before the waters behind John Day rose in this area, and there were no dangerous rapids. Alder Creek was a favorite crossing place for Indians, who swam their horses and carried their bundles in canoes. Lewis and Clark camped here with Indians one night. One of the members of the expedition had brought his violin, and to satisfy the Indians' curiosity, the instrument was tuned up and "some of the men amused themselves with dancing."

Quesnel Park, located in a small inlet at the mouth of Threemile Canyon on the south shore, is considered a good place from which to water-ski. There is a boat ramp and facilities for overnight camping and trailers, but no hookups. The canyon's name reflects the early settlers' pragmatic view of life in keeping with this stark and unadorned locale: the canyon is, logically, three miles from Willow Creek.

West of the park, Willow Creek empties into the Columbia at Heppner Junction, Oregon. It flows down through dry hills with flattened tops. Looking up the creek, you see a broad inlet with sloping sides that provide protection from the winds. But here, as at many coves along the river, the entrance is passable only by small boats. Two highway bridges and a railroad bridge span the creek, all with a vertical clearance of ten feet.

In the summer the creek is usually placid, as it was early on a Sunday in June 1903. But that afternoon the worst tragedy on a tributary of the Columbia took place. A cloudburst caused a flash flood that transformed the Balm Fork of Willow Creek near Heppner, forty-two miles inland, from a creek eight feet wide and a foot deep to a raging river. It wiped out Heppner, taking 225 lives in less than twenty minutes.

For the first time since leaving the basalt corridor of Wallula Gap, you begin again to feel as if you are sailing through a mountain pass. Ridges build on the Oregon side, and the mountains on the Washington side are steep and massive. Slopes are still treeless. Even Lewis and Clark made note of this in 1805 when they camped just above Roosevelt, Washington: "not a tree to be seen in any direction except a few small willow bushes which are scattered partially on the sides of the banks."

Looking down river you will see a large headland on the north shore. Below it on a broad bench stands the small railroad hamlet of Roosevelt. Slightly down river is Roosevelt Park, and across from it is Arlington, Oregon. They mark the end of your cruise through desert and irrigated fields.

To find Roosevelt Park, watch for rock jetties and a green marker. Although located in a slightly wind-exposed area, the park offers solitude away from towns. Besides moorage, there is also a launch

*Roosevelt Park*

ramp and dock, but no gas or supplies. The green lawns, restrooms, sandy swimming beach, and playground are not unusual in a park. What is unexpected is the large boulder that was carried from British Columbia by the Spokane floods near the end of the last Ice Age.

The last ferry to operate on this part of the river crossed between the site of the park and Arlington. A sign in the park still points the way to the old ferry landing.

Arlington's waterfront has been extended by building a jetty into the river. Silos stand on top, and the moorage is tucked inside. The town fans out from the mouth of Alkali Canyon, with homes scattered about on the gently sloped walls. For four years, beginning in 1881, Arlington was named Alkali for the extensive alkali deposits located nearby. During a town meeting, N. A. Cornish suggested that a new and more delicate name be chosen, and proposed Arlington in honor of the southerners who lived there. His real motivation for the name change was not learned until years later, when Cornish's daughter

*Arlington, Oregon*

revealed that her father's middle name was Arlington.

Entrance to the moorage is a well-defined, dredged channel on the downriver side of the jetty. It is a good haven from the winds. The waterway extends toward town under the highway bridge—vertical clearance ten feet—and into the city park, where a beach rims shallow water where children can swim. There is also a boat launch ramp. From the outside moorage it is a short, pleasant walk to Arlington's two-block shopping area, complete with restaurants, service stations, and motels.

On this cruise, unobstructed by dams, you have remained at the same elevation, 265 feet above sea level, as the river has coursed its way across the plainslike region of desert and irrigated fields. Although Cruise Five is only a few miles longer, you'll be quite aware of its descent through the Cascades. You lock-through two dams, John Day and The Dalles, and arrive at 72 feet above sea level.

# Cruise
# Five

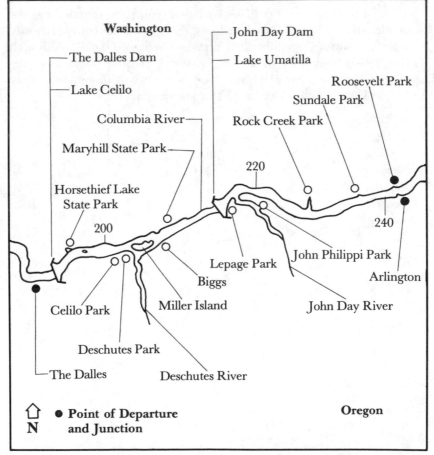

Washington

The Dalles Dam

Lake Celilo

Columbia River

Maryhill State Park

Horsethief Lake
State Park

200

Celilo Park

Deschutes Park

The Dalles

John Day Dam

Lake Umatilla

Roosevelt Park

Sundale Park

Rock Creek Park

220

Lepage Park

Biggs

Miller Island

Deschutes River

John Philippi Park

John Day River

240

Arlington

Oregon

N

● Point of Departure
and Junction

*Do not use for navigation.*
*Use NOAA Nautical Charts 18536, 18535, and 18533*

# Roosevelt and Arlington to The Dalles

**Point of departure:** Roosevelt Park, Washington; Arlington, Oregon

**Course:** Columbia River via Lake Umatilla and John Day Lock and Dam with a vertical drop of 105 feet, and Lake Celilo and The Dalles Lock and Dam with a vertical drop of 88 feet to Lake Bonneville

**Stops:** Sundale Park, Rock Creek Park, Lepage Park, John Philippi Park, Maryhill State Park, Deschutes State Park, Miller Island, Celilo Park, The Dalles

**Length of cruise:** approximately 50 statute miles

**Duration on power:** 1 day

**Duration on sail:** 2 to 3 days

**Overnight moorage:** Rock Creek Park, Lepage Park, John Philippi Park, The Dalles

**Junction point for Cruise Six:** The Dalles, Oregon

# Cruising over History

For most boaters, it is what you are actually passing by that catches your attention. Yet on this reach of the river, there is an additional source of interest. Here, more than on any other part of the inland waterway, the impounded waters cover remnants of history both ancient and modern. By reading depths on the chart, you can discover traces of the drop of old Celilo Falls near Wishram, the canal used by riverboats along the south shore near Brown's Island, and the Long Narrows, a deep chute and rapids above The Dalles Lock and Dam where hundreds of Indians from distant tribes once gathered for trade and festivities. Because these vestiges are no longer evident as you cruise by, we will dip at times into this river of the past as we go along.

As you move out in the morning, you may be the first boat to cut a design in the still water, and the only one to do so for an hour or two. The sky is brushed with drifting clouds creating a wash in shades of brown from the river to the surrounding cliffs and hills. A stroke of color appears about five miles down river at Sundale Park on the north shore. The park can be distinguished by the rectangular patterns of poplars and orchards green in the summer and gray in the winter on the barren hillside.

Chapman Creek, named for the settler who first planted orchards here, flows through the trees, forming a small lake at the park. This sheltered cove is a good place to duck out of gusty winds or, later in the day, to unpack the fixings for a picnic in the shade. There is a boat launch and a tie-up dock. The clearance of the railroad bridge at the entrance is twenty-nine feet.

Although a sense of isolation prevails here today, at one time during the 1800s it was more active, when a ferry carried cowboys from Chapman Creek to a saloon at Blalock, Oregon, downstream. At Lang Canyon, across from Sundale Park, riverboats stopped to take on loads of wool sent down from the hills above by way of a tram.

Through this wide, straight stretch the winds may kick up unexpectedly and create what one boat crew called "scrambled-eggs water." During a summer cruise anticipating no great change on the river, they started fixing breakfast. Eggs cooking in a pan suddenly decorated the walls of the galley—not once, but twice—before skipper and cook agreed that preparations should stop.

Between Sundale Park and Rock Creek along the north shore, the river covers the first remnant of history on this cruise—Fountain Bar. The bar, once two miles long, was one of the most populous Indian communities on the mid-Columbia River. For fifty years before parts of the bar were blasted, then covered by water, collectors dug and sifted through sands and found many relics. One small bit of Fountain Bar is occasionally exposed; a black buoy just above the mouth of Rock Creek marks this spot as a hazard to navigation. Near this point is a submerged fish lead constructed by the Indians. The stone structure guided salmon to a low cliff where the Indians dipped them from the water with nets.

Lewis and Clark camped just above Rock Creek on their cross-country return in April 1806. Their terse description gives a sketch of the river and people then: "Continued our march along narrow, rocky bottom on north side of river about twelve miles to Wah-how-pum village of twelve mat lodges near the Rock rapids."

Rock Creek flows through a canyon by a quiet and secluded park about a mile in from the river. A favorite spot for trout fishermen and bird hunters, Rock Creek Park includes a sandy-bottom swimming area, picnic tables, gazebos, a boat launch, and restrooms. Highway and railroad bridges, each with a vertical clearance of twenty-four feet, cross the entrance, which leads into a small cove. When you move up the creek, you may feel pinched by the dry, barren walls, but the depths are good and the canyon widens at the park.

Below Rock Creek, the river starts a long, sweeping bend, and a climate change begins to be barely perceptible. The desert is softened by small collections of low, pale green ground cover, and the first trees can be seen growing on high ridges. The few scattered ponderosa pine and juniper hold tightly to the thin soil. This transition is gradual, for the desert keeps its tenacious hold for some distance yet down river.

At the end of the bend, Oregon's John Day River and John Day Lock and Dam come into view. If you are able to move under the bridges (vertical clearance nineteen feet) crossing the John Day River, there are two parks, and both are recommended stops. Near the bridges, Lepage Park offers levels of manicured lawns, shade trees, a buoy-protected swim area, a well-designed boat ramp, and a water-ski dock. This is an excellent in and out place for the trailer-boater to explore the Columbia or to make the fifteen-minute run up the John Day River to John Philippi Park, which is accessible only by boat.

The channel to the park cuts between dry hills, and you cannot help but be struck by the contrast between the water and the parched land of its banks. A few range cattle glance up bemused by the sound of a powerboat in the otherwise silent canyon. Paths of spring tributaries

*John Philippi Park on the John Day River*

are marked by slight green veins of growth. There is no hint of the park until you are almost upon it. Like the proverbial oasis, it sits in royal green isolation. A boomed swimming area with a good sandy beach is available, with sturdy cement docks just beyond. No water or electricity is available at the dock area, but ingenious vacationers bring extension cords and plug into electricity from the main shower facility. On one trip we saw some yachting club members on a week's vacation use a small deep freeze to provide an important requirement in the summer-time heat — a steady supply of ice. Hoses can also be strung to the dock area.

This is truly the poor man's Palm Springs of the Northwest. On weekends the area is crowded with noisy drag boaters. Usually, pleasure boaters leave and go to some Columbia River port for overnight. Yet we have stayed through the weekend and found the influx of new boaters interesting. If you are a people-watcher and enjoy talking about powerboats, it can be a very pleasant experience.

The lawns are extensive and can be used for tenting, but one note of warning: take time to read the computerized watering schedule posted on the showerhouse walls. Otherwise, you may be an unwitting participant in middle-of-the-night slapstick, when the large sprinkler heads that have been hidden by lush grass suddenly pop up spewing water. Invariably, they pop up directly under the canvas floor of some unsuspecting camper, or else water collects and runs downhill into some other naive tenter's homebase. So check the schedule and set your tent accordingly.

One excellent side trip is a slow amble up the narrowing channel to the rocks of the rapids marking the end of the backwater. Along the way, the water creates tiny coves as it reaches into the soft curves of the hillsides. By tying to an old tree on land or dropping the hook in the soft mud of the bank, you can block off a small cove with your boat. Your only company is the ruminating cow blinking her soft brown eyes at such goings-on. Hence, you can enjoy a luxurious skinny-dipping afternoon in the tepid water.

At the park, however, do not let the resort atmosphere lull you into forgetting the realities of the land. There are signs warning you to watch out for rattlesnakes. And sudden afternoon thundershowers occur now and then. On more than one occasion we have taken families on board after late evening winds have swept down the desert gullies and blown their tents over. The winds present few problems for boats, however, as there is little fetch for wave action to build and the moorages are secure.

The confluence of the Columbia and John Day rivers is about a mile above the dam. Across and down from this point the cliffs appear like a crumbling fortress, contrasting sharply with the precise, concrete lines of the dam's structure. This dam and the river were named after a Virginia backwoodsman who traveled with the Astor-Hunt overland party in 1811. John Day and a companion were robbed of everything they owned, including their clothing, by hostile Indians near the mouth of the river now bearing his name. As early as 1825, the name John Day's River began to appear in explorers' journals.

Just above the dam on the Washington side, a large modern structure standing by itself seems out of place. This is the Commonwealth Aluminum Plant, which was built next to the dam to use some of its power. John Day Dam was completed in 1968, and is the newest of the four locks and dams on the Columbia River portion of the inland waterway.

Approach the lock, located on the north side, with caution. A lighted buoy with a sign marks rocks that are awash or at water level. One boater misread the marker, hit the rocks, and was delayed for four days waiting for repairs.

The locking time is usually faster than on some other locks, and averages twenty minutes. You will note that the lower gates, like those at Lower Monumental and Ice Harbor, open upward, lifted by huge cables from towers. These are the highest (113 feet) single-lift locks in the Western world. If you should lock-through with a commercial tug and wheat barge, you will be with part of the 200,000 tons of grain that move down the Columbia each month.

When you emerge from the lock, keep a firm grip on the tiller or wheel. Here, as at other locks, the water running out creates a

*Navigation lock at John Day Lock and Dam*

whirlpool, and this area is marked "dangerous." Keep clear of it, then follow the marked channel. A shoaly area lies in the middle of the river below the dam.

Soon the current slows and the water again takes on the character of a lake. This one is Lake Celilo, which takes its name from the falls now covered by the lake. Several origins have been suggested for the name Celilo. The most likely is that it is the Yakima word for "cleft in the bank." The lake is twenty-nine miles long and 160 feet above sea level. Because the water level can fluctuate 5 feet in one day, be sure to have adequate depth beneath the keel if you anchor out.

During the summer, an afternoon squall may occasionally blow, but rarely are there more than two days in a row of bad weather.

One day when we traveled this way, the sun was near its zenith, the river—again on a straight course—looked like a band of hammered pewter passing through cliffs and plateaus. We looked up to see Mount Hood at the end of the band, its flanks still covered with snow.

For nearly the next one hundred miles, as you follow the winding river through the Cascades and down to the eastern edge of the Coast range, Mount Hood seems like a pivotal point. It is not always in sight, but each time it appears it seems to be in a different location, with a different face and a different landscape spreading below it.

Down river, near the end of the straight passage, a highway bridge spans the river connecting the communities of Biggs, Oregon, and Maryhill, Washington. Though sparsely populated, this area has become well known—not for its scenic grandeur but for the grand ideas of one man, Sam Hill, a multimillionaire and the son-in-law of James Hill, the railroad tycoon.

Sam Hill's grand ideas can be seen in the two monuments he built on bluffs high above the river's north shore: Stonehenge, east of the bridge above the town of Maryhill, and the Maryhill Museum, down river from the bridge. Stonehenge is a replica of the druid temple in England, and was built as a World War I memorial. Its gray stone walls with hollow doors were the site of reenacted druid ceremonies during the eclipse that momentarily darkened Washington in 1979. The buff colored walls of the Maryhill Museum blend with the hillside where it stands nine hundred feet above the river. Remaining true to his style and grand ideas, Hill invited Queen Marie of Rumania to dedicate the museum, and she did so in 1926. It is now filled with historic pieces from European collections and from this area, including two Lewis and Clark silver peace medals.

Unfortunately, neither of these intriguing monuments is easily accessible to boaters. You can tie up at the beautiful Maryhill State Park along the river's edge, but the location of the museum and Stonehenge requires a long hike up steep hills. In addition to a boat launch, a swimming beach, and picnic tables, there is an old locomotive on the park grounds. This is a good place to get out of the sun and let the river breezes cool you.

This area bears memories of the harsh early days. Above Biggs is a canyon called "Spanish Hollow," named to commemorate the death of a Spanish ox, a small catastrophe during the settlers' immigration. Looking down the Oregon side, you can imagine how inspiring this view was in the 1840s for the overland settlers coming through the break in the hills. It marks the place along the Oregon Trail where the Columbia River first came into view.

Another Indian site, this one above water, is on Miller Island. On this large island in the next bend of the river, archeologists found 132 house-pits. These pits, four feet deep, were part of semisubterranean Indian houses. Archeologists also found many artifacts, and red petroglyphs drawn on rock shelters. Later on, the house-pits were filled in and the island seeded to summer pasture for cattle. A hook in the upper end of Miller Island forms a cove for anchoring. Although the wider channel swings south of the island by the mouth of the Deschutes River, a second and more interesting channel, called Hell's Gate, follows the north side through a narrow, high-walled passage. Suddenly you are in a miniature gorge, where you may see deer and other wild-life. Often the deer are strangely unwilling to run. An idling boat will draw their attention, and they pause to stare curiously at you. This short cut, besides being interesting, may provide a respite from buf-feting winds blowing in the south channel. If you encounter winds in the south channel, you can duck into Deschutes State Park and Camp-ground near the mouth of the Deschutes River. The bridge's vertical clearance is twenty feet.

From the river's curve below Miller Island you can see Wishram, Washington. On the rocks around Wishram are Indian petroglyphs of god, sun, and totem designs. On the low bench, railcars are strung out in front of houses crowded between tall poplar windbreaks. Newer homes are scattered on terraces above. Once the largest railyards on the Spokane, Portland and Seattle Railroad, it now serves the Burlington Northern Railroad.

Directly across the river is a large recreational spot, Celilo Park. In the summer it is a favorite place for water-skiers, swimmers, boaters, and picnickers. There is a boat launch, and some Indians still use a small dock area here to unload their few salmon.

Had you sailed this way sixty years ago, the scene and activity would have been quite different. Shelves of dark rock stretched across the river. In the dry season, the water ran down the deep cracks, but during spring runoff, the river plunged over the rocks, creating Celilo Falls. Indians stood on flimsy platforms that hung out over the churn-ing water as they dipped their nets to catch salmon.

Near Celilo Park, huge wheels hung in scaffolding creaked as they turned and scooped up salmon from the river. The salmon were then processed in a cannery nearby. Below the park, you might have seen a steamboat or gas-powered boat emerge from Celilo Canal. The wheels, the falls, the canal, and their remnants are now submerged.

Fishwheels operated along the banks of the Columbia on both the Oregon and Washington shores for over forty years. These ingenious contraptions scooped up salmon by the ton as they returned to their spawning grounds. On one day in May 1913, a fishwheel located above The Dalles scooped up the record catch for fishwheels—thirty-five tons. Seventy-nine stationary wheels dotted the river's edge from the present Celilo Park to several miles below Bonneville Dam. As a con-servation measure they were voted out of existence in Oregon in 1926 and in Washington a few years later.

The once-exposed rock, rapids, and falls through the ten-mile reach between Celilo Park and The Dalles created travel problems for early settlers. They solved these in the mid-1800s by building a portage railroad. Passengers disembarked from steamboats at The Dalles and

*Indians fishing at Celilo Falls in 1951*

transferred to the railroad. Up river, they boarded another steamer. But steamboat companies wanted passage for their boats around the rapids. Work began once Congress provided the money to build a canal, and for over eight years workmen blasted and drilled a path through the rock. Finally completed in 1916, Celilo Canal was eight miles long. About the same time, however, river traffic began to decline and the canal was little used.

Even though the rapids and their hazards now lie submerged, wind hazards can cause difficulty through this area. Often the water is blown into a foaming series of short, steep waves. The railroad bridge ahead, its piers embedded in rock, has a clearance of twenty feet, and a lift span for boats requiring more clearance.

Beyond the bridge, the elongated form of Horsethief Butte, collapsed in the middle, stands out above the north shore. Beneath it a lake lying in a swale sloping toward the river is the site of Horsethief Lake State Park. The lake, banked with trees, is not accessible to river traffic, although there is a launch ramp between the railroad tracks and the river. The park is located at the head of the submerged Long Narrows, also known as the Grand Dalles, and Five-Mile Rapids. Here the river was suddenly compressed into a basalt channel about two hundred feet wide. For thousands of years the location of the present park was a favorite congregating place for Indians, and was considered the great trading mart of the West. Canoe paddlers from the coast, nomads from east of the Cascades, seed-eaters from the Great Basin, and buffalo hunters from the plains met here. Most came to gamble, trade, and enjoy the festivities. Some came to fish. The fish were easily caught with a spear or net, then smoked over coals and packed in baskets lined with leaves.

One of the largest Indian mounds excavated along the Columbia was Wakemap Mound, which now lies mostly submerged, west of the park. Thousands of artifacts were uncovered, and a complete record of Indians dating back two thousand years was compiled before the mound was inundated.

The Dalles Dam gates closed on 10 March 1957, and in four hours and forty-five minutes the waters covered all physical traces of former Indian life—their fishing grounds, the creaking fishwheels, and the rapids that vexed early travelers.

As you move over the past, you approach the present—The Dalles Lock and Dam. It is fitting that the dam carries the name of a geographical feature that affected the lives of so many people. The locks are located next to the Washington shore. There is a small cove just above the lock, should you have to wait. As you lock-through, you will easily and quietly move over what once took master navigation skills to maneuver. The gates that help make this possible are over one hundred feet tall and weigh 350 tons. The drop is eighty-eight feet.

When exiting onto Lake Bonneville, check your chart and note the navigation markers on the rocks and rapids. There is a strong current here, and you need to be alert and maintain a good speed forward. As one boater noted, "If you're not paying attention, you can lose it here." No matter how good the weather, the water is rarely smooth at this point.

The power lines that can be seen going up and across the hill on the Oregon side are headed toward the world's largest operating converter station, which converts the AC current from the dam to DC for transfer over the world's largest transmission lines.

The river swings in a loop around a wide, sloping plateau to the north. To the south, the town of The Dalles begins on a narrow shore, then its ordered streets ascend the hills beyond. You will see an impressive array of textures and shapes from this vantage point. Vertical basalt banks contain the river. Wharves, warehouses, and silos extend along the waterfront. Rising above the downtown rooftops is the red brick spire on Saint Peter's Church, built in 1897. A six-foot high rooster stands on top of the spire. On the ridges above, ponderosa pine are interspersed with Douglas fir—the leading edge of what will become dense forests.

An overnight stop at the Port of The Dalles Marina is a perfect ending to a cruise over history. The moorage, down river from the highway bridge and in front of town, is well protected, the entrance easily located and navigated. Gas and water are available here, and if you need to replenish foodstuffs on board, a grocery store is within walking distance.

The distance to town is too far to be a pleasant stroll, but you can catch a ride with someone going that way or call the taxi service. The town and its history are worth investigating. You might consider a visit to the Fort Dalles Museum and the park area at the "End of the Oregon Trail." The museum, up the hill about fourteen blocks from the middle of town, is housed in the old surgeon's quarters, and is the only remaining building of Fort Dalles. The Fort began as a primitive stockade in 1847, but was turned into a showplace by Captain Thomas Jordon, who arrived in 1856. A man of luxurious tastes, he spent large amounts of the government's money building ornate houses.

The Dalles was especially important during the steamboat era. In 1850, the town began to move ahead, but it was not until the gold rush of 1860 in eastern Oregon and Idaho that The Dalles boomed. It became the prime outfitting and "jump off point" for the miners. Historians record twenty-five saloons filled with miners awaiting steamboat passage to the up river goldfields.

Sitting on the stern in the blue haze of evening, watching the panorama of mountains and river, you can almost imagine the aroma of Indian fires smoking salmon, and the pioneers' howls of celebration after they had run the Long Narrows and pulled safely ashore.

Yet, for those continuing down river, more rapids lay ahead in the deeper canyons of the Columbia Gorge. Cruise Six takes you into these canyons and into the heart of the gorge.

# Cruise
# Six

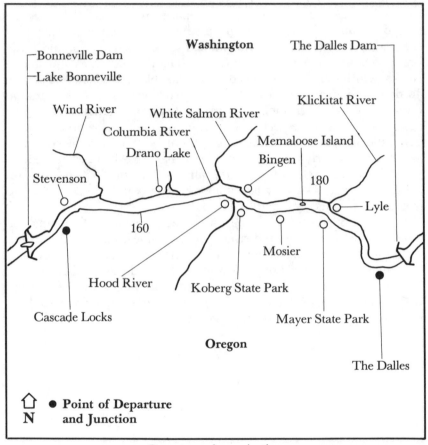

Do not use for navigation.
Use NOAA Nautical Chart 18531

# The Dalles
# to Cascade Locks

**Point of departure:** The Dalles, Oregon

**Course:** Columbia River via Lake Bonneville

**Stops:** Mayer State Park, Koberg Beach State Park, Bingen Boat Basin, Hood River, Drano Lake, Wind River, Government Cove, Stevenson, Cascade Locks

**Length of cruise:** approximately 40 statute miles

**Duration on power:** 1 day

**Duration on sail:** 2 days

**Overnight moorage:** Bingen Boat Basin, Hood River, Stevenson, Cascade Locks

**Junction point for Cruise Seven:** Cascade Locks, Oregon

# The Heart of the Columbia Gorge

Tree-covered mountain walls thrust above the winding river. Early morning mists drift among the folded slopes. Orchards heavy with fruit line small valleys that fan out beyond the river. Waterfalls leap into space. This is the heart of the Columbia Gorge—forty miles ahead on Lake Bonneville. The length and boundaries of the gorge vary, depending on whom you ask. Some say it extends from Crown Point above Portland to Arlington, others say it reaches from the Sandy River to the Deschutes River, a distance of about one hundred miles. Regardless of the length or the boundaries, no one disputes the beauty of the gorge.

But another kind of dispute is building. This one is over future land use within the gorge. Commissions are being formed and studies undertaken to plan which lands are to be preserved and which are to be developed to accommodate growth. It is possible that part of the region will eventually be designated a National Scenic Area.

With no dam blocking this cruise, your planning will not need to include the time allowed to lock-through. The last dam as you descend the inland waterway is Bonneville, a few miles below Cascade Locks. Your planning might include stops at waterway parks, however, or visits to resort towns.

The vanguards of the Cascade range forests can be seen on the slopes above The Dalles. Ponderosa pine is the predominant species, with Douglas fir bunched in the draws where more moisture collects. Their branches and tops cant toward the east, giving testimony to the westerlies that are common in the gorge. This forest and that to the west provided fuel for the river's steamboats and work for early settlers. Firewood for paddlewheelers was delivered by sailing scows to the beach near the mouth of Miller Creek west of The Dalles.

The scows, often owned and run by families, were flat, bargelike boats with a large sail. Occasionally, a small cabin aft served as living quarters for the family. One local historian recalled seeing a scow with a cow tied at the stern. "It provided fresh milk for the family," he explained. Wind pushed the scows, with their loads of forty to eighty cords of wood, up river to The Dalles. When the wind dropped, an anchor was thrown out to hold the scow in place against the river's current. On the return trip, water sails were rigged. Sacks of rocks were hung on each clew and with the sail were lowered into the water. The current then pushed against the sail, carrying the scow downstream. The cordwood business dwindled after the turn of the century, and the fleet of sailing scows disappeared from the river as coal-burning loco-motives replaced the steamboats.

As you leave The Dalles, you move through one of the narrowest parts of the Columbia River. For a short distance the river is pinched between low cliffs as it swings north. The river's depth here ranges from 52 to 150 feet. Beyond the curve at Squally Point, the river opens wide and flows past the Paha cliffs in Washington. These perpendicular walls of lava rock are notable not for their height but for their sym-metry: they look as if they had been shaped by a carver working with ruler and square. Indian legends have their own explanation: the coyote god turned both humans and animals into these pillars of stone.

Steady or gusting winds are common here, as they are elsewhere in the gorge. Local boaters recommend that should you be on the water when the wind comes up, throttling the boat down just enough to maintain way will alleviate the banging or jarring ride. Or, you can travel closer to shore in safe depths, or find a moorage to protect you from the wind. Mayer State Park, on the Oregon shore across from Lyle, is one such haven out of the wind—and a pleasant stop in any weather.

A narrow entrance opens into a small shallow bay. Having navigated it past old pilings (most are gone now) at dusk, we know it is possible to pick your way into the bay. Small boats can also be launched here from a ramp. This large park, where broad lawns are shaded by trees, is for day use. There are swimming and boating areas, picnic tables, stoves and restroom facilities with a bathhouse. The water is warm—our children have enjoyed swimming and sunning there. If you are using the park as a haven from the wind, periodically nose your boat out of the bay to test the wind and water of the channel, since there is no way of appraising the situation from inside. Water levels can fluc-tuate up to four feet behind the Bonneville Dam, and such a drop could isolate a fixed-keel sailboat. Even if you had an easy entrance, you will not be able to exit when the water drops. In this case, you simply wait for the water to rise.

Across the river is the small town of Lyle. For a long time it was the terminus of the Columbia River and Northern Railroad, and a shipping point for a farm and orchard district located in the hills beyond. The main part of town lies along the highway, but the hotel that served travelers when the train stopped regularly can be seen above the railroad tracks. There is one unmaintained boat ramp down river from the hotel.

West of town the Klickitat River flows into the Columbia, its clear waters slowly spreading out, then mixing with the brown-shaded waters of the Columbia. Stay south of the day marker that indicates the shoals around the mouth of the river.

One of the most famous vault burial islands used by the Indians is Memaloose Island, named Sepulcher Island by Lewis and Clark. This desolate piece of basalt is located near the center of the river just below Chatfield, Oregon. Memaloose, a name common to many islands and rocks in the river, is from the Chinook jargon for the dead. The large white monument that stands on the island commemorates Vic Trevett, a pioneer of The Dalles. One night Trevett was drinking in a saloon with his friends, Amos Underwood and John Martin. They began talking about death, and made a pact that they all would be buried on the island. Trevett said he wanted to sleep among honest people. He was the only one whose friends and relatives honored the pact, and he was buried on Memaloose Island in 1883.

You can anchor on the west end of the island, but watch out for long sandbars. Avoid anchoring too close to the south side. The channel here is narrow and large barge tows pass very close to the island.

Below Memaloose Island the river carves a broad sweep between hills sloping gently to the river. Cupped among the hills on the Oregon shore is Mosier, with orchards growing behind. The town was established in 1853 by J.H. Mosier and for a while was called Mosier Landing. The first school was attended by Mosier's twelve children and three other children who lived in Washington territory. They rowed across the Columbia each day to attend class.

Although you have come only about twenty miles on this cruise, you might consider one of three places ahead for a stop. All are gathered beneath high mountains. Like choosing delicacies from a smorgasbord, each offers something for the individual taste. You can swim at Koberg Beach State Park, Oregon, away from crowds, walk through Bingen, Washington, a Bavarian style town, or dine in elegant style at a twenties-vintage hotel in Hood River, Oregon.

The east side of Koberg Beach State Park at Stanley Rock will accommodate fixed-keel vessels. From here you can dinghy in for swimming and picnicking in an area well protected from westerly winds. Powerboats or swing-keel boats may choose the west end of the rock, where the beach is shallower and good for swimming or water-skiing.

Some of the earliest settlements in the heart of the gorge were located in the White Salmon, Bingen, and Hood River areas. The mild climate and fertile soils attracted early pioneers to the valley between Mount Hood and the Columbia. The first settlers arrived at Hood River in the 1850s, and the Joslyn family established an orchard and farm on the present site of Bingen in 1853. Though they were burned

*Hood River Valley and Mount Hood*

out in the Indian uprising of 1855–56, the Joslyn family escaped and returned to build a home, which still stands. Joslyn later sold out to two brothers from Germany, who in 1892 laid out a town on the property and called it Bingen because the location reminded them of Bingen on the Rhine River.

The first apple orchards were planted in Hood River Valley in 1895, and produce-bearing acreage continued to expand on both sides of the river after that. At one time, two hundred acres of strawberries were planted near White Salmon.

Even though the river separated them, the settlers on both sides mingled as friends and neighbors. They crossed the river—which was sometimes filled with ice in harsh winters—in their crude boats to trade goods, celebrate holidays together, and worship on Sundays. Later on, sail-powered ferries crossed the river. One skipper, Captain Stanley, sailed between Koberg's beach and Bingen. Another ferry crossing was run by Captain Amos Underwood, whose two sailboats operated between Hood River and Underwood, Washington.

These two captains used the winds to earn a living. They and their ferries are gone, but the winds continue to blow. Sailors used the winds for racing, and recently, another group discovered these winds. During summer months, wind surfers sail the gorge for fun and competition in international meets.

While racers and wind surfers seek the winds, others prefer to get out of them. A haven from strong westerlies is the Bingen Boat Basin. Its entrance is near marker three. Concrete docks, a ramp, picnic tables, and restrooms provide a pleasant place for a short stop or a place to tie up while you walk into Bingen.

Storefronts are decorated in Bavarian style, and near the west end of town there is an antique store, a winery, and a bed and breakfast. Now called The Grand Old House, it was built by the Joslyn family in 1860.

Other bed and breakfast lodgings located in this area of the gorge are listed in the back of the book.

The town of Hood River offers some of the most tourist-oriented moorages on the river. An active Chamber of Commerce works hard to make tourism, including boating, a part of the economy. Another part is the fruit business: packing houses process apples, pears, and other fruit grown in Hood River Valley, and logos designed with fruit symbols are used liberally by local businesses.

The boat basin is just down river from the highway bridge crossing the Columbia. Here at Mid-Columbia Marina, part of the Port of Hood River, you will find overnight moorage, water, gas, diesel, a ramp, and boat repairs. If fishing is on your mind, these waters include sturgeon year-round, steelhead and salmon in spring and fall. For local "holes," check at sport supply stores.

The boat basin is part of an attractively designed waterfront complex, and includes a large parking lot for trailers and recreational vehicles. A stretch of sandy river beach includes a sailboard park and a swimming area with barbecues and picnic tables nearby. After a swim and time on the sand, you can wash off the grit in showers located in the restroom facilities.

In the visitors' center, note the relief maps of the river, which will give you an excellent feel for this location in the gorge. Bits and pieces of local history are also on display.

Part of this waterfront complex includes the Hood River Village and Hood River Inn east of the basin. Here you can meander through an art gallery and shops, or enjoy a meal served in the dining room at the inn. From the dining room facing the river you can watch boats sailing by and look up to the steep ridges of White Salmon, where homes are perched along the edges.

Getting into town to buy groceries or liquor is usually a matter of hitching a ride or calling for taxi service. Although the walk is long, it is not impossible. You may be able to get a ride with someone going into town by inquiring at the Chamber of Commerce office in the basin building. If you are in town on Wednesday and want a real treat, try Bette's Place, a local cafe. It is open all week, but on Wednesdays the specialty is cinnamon rolls.

One place we have enjoyed and highly recommend is the Columbia Gorge Hotel. Try it for dinner, Saturday or Sunday brunch, or an overnight stay. As it is not a place for jeans and tennis shoes, you'll want to save some of your vacation funds and one pair of clean "duds" for this part of the trip. It's worth it!

Built in 1920 as an extravagant tourist resort, the hotel overlooks the river from a cliff west of town. Restored in 1979 to its original design, it exudes a sense of elegance. Evening drinks or morning coffee may be enjoyed in a comfortable drawing room in front of a fire. As you savor a gourmet meal in the dining room you will have a view of the river and of blowing trees on steep-sided mountains.

Before leaving, be sure to take a walk through the hotel grounds. The stonework of walks and small bridges shows the meticulous workmanship of those earlier years. A creek flows through the grounds, and falls plunge over the cliff almost directly outside the dining room windows. The small pool and marsh below are home to a few ducks.

For a ride to the hotel, call (503)386-5566. A black limousine will arrive to take you up the hill.

If you have spent a night on your boat you may look out in the morning and see wind beating the river into waves, the spray flying from their crests. Pulling your head in, you may tell the crew, "We'll stay another day and wait this out." Yet, at the same time, sailors clad in yellow slickers clamber on their sailboats. They uncover the sails, check the rigging, and one by one move out on the river. Sailors here love the wind—so much so that, as a sailing club member said, "We call a race if the winds are twenty knots or less." One regatta, called the "Race Through the Mountains," was held when sixty-mile-an-hour gusts were blowing. One skipper said that as the winds screamed, he kept looking up from troughs to see only the masts of the other boats.

But there are calm days and light breezy days here, too. As you leave Hood River in the morning, the air is cool in the shadows of this deep mountain pass. Filmy strands of clouds like cobwebs brush the boat's mast or bridge and whirl about as the boat moves through them and onto the river. Gradually, as the sun's rays push away the shadows, the clouds vanish.

Poised on a rock jetty across the river from the boat basin, the Spring Creek Fish Hatchery looks like a new marina. It was the first salmon hatchery on the Columbia River, but with the addition of automated equipment it is now the newest and most modern.

From mid-channel you see falls plunging down the cliff near the bright orange Columbia Gorge Hotel. These are among the first of many falls you will see on both sides of the gorge to its end about forty miles downstream. Each one has its own pristine quality: some are narrow wisps during the rainy season and are gone in the summer; others, such as Multnomah Falls, attract crowds in all seasons.

Though not of nature's creation, there is something else to watch for on the Washington side. The wooden legs and trough of a lumber flume owned by Broughton Lumber Company cling tightly to the mountains' contours west of Underwood. The owners feel that this old flume, the last of many used on the west coast from the late 1800s to early 1900s, is still the most efficient way to transport lumber the nine miles from the sawmill to the finishing plant at Underwood.

Even though rapids in the gorge no longer offer the adventure and thrills of travel that they did fifty years ago, the river's path has changed little over recent centuries. Following it, you slip beneath Underwood Mountain and the White Salmon volcano, both quiescent volcanoes, then past the flanks of mountains such as Wind and Shellrock. Along the edge of this path, spring brings delicate green tracery to the trees and bushes. In the fall, they turn to crimson and burnt orange.

One place to stop and enjoy this area away from towns is Drano Lake on the north shore. The name, as some have said, is not fitting to the beauty of the location. Once a bay before the railroad filled in front of it, the lake was named for William Drano, an early settler. Unfortunately the lake is off-limits to boats that need more than a nineteen-foot clearance, since a railroad and highway bridge span the entrance.

The Little White Salmon River drains into the lake. One of the oldest national fish hatcheries is located near the mouth of this river, where Chinook, coho, and chum salmon are raised. In the fall, you can watch salmon spawning in the river. You can tie up near the boat launch or to log rafts stored on the lake. This is a good wind-sheltered area.

Collins Point, about two miles down river near the eastern side of Wind Mountain, is marked by two interesting geological areas. This is an active slide area, and movement in some areas is forty-five feet per year. It is also the beginning of a hot springs zone that runs ten miles to the west.

Evidence of the slide area below Collins Point can be seen from the river: the soil is buckled, and trees stand at an odd angle. This slide covers about three square miles, reaching up onto the mountain slopes. Bonneville power lines were once strung across the upper part of the slide. As the earth moved, the towers moved, and workmen made repairs and realignments many times before relocating them.

Early entrepreneurs, recognizing the curative and cash value of hot springs, built hotels and resorts around them. Shipards Hot Springs and St. Martin's Hot Springs were located at Carson, Washington. Possibly one of the largest and most popular was Collins Hot Springs near Collins Point, the remnants of which are now under water. It started out as a bathhouse with five wooden tubs about 1900. Steamboats brought customers, and the business and facilities grew to include a hotel and a bathhouse with ninety-six rooms. James Attwell, a local historian, wrote: "Guests arrived on every steamboat. Wealthy businessmen often brought office girls when their wives were not along."

Beyond Wind and Shellrock mountains, the river opens wide as it curves past the mouth of Wind River on the north. A protected area lies behind the fill for the highway and railroad. Clearance under the bridges is twenty-six feet. Log rafts are stored inside, and there is an unimproved boat ramp and a wobbly dock. Watch for small reefs outside the entrance. Just west of the entrance on the Columbia River side is a small cove with deep water, providing a haven for larger boats. Another protected spot is Government Cove down river on the Oregon shore. The entrance is southwest of red buoy number eighteen.

Today the river here is wide. The rapids, sand, and gravel bars and rocks are covered by slack water, and navigation is not as hazardous as it was when steamboats traveled this way. It took a skillful captain to negotiate the combination of currents and winds and maneuver between rocks just wide enough for a steamboat to pass. There were no U.S. Coast Guard aids to navigation, no lighted buoys for night running. The captains relied on knowledge developed through experience. Especially when running at night, they depended on the tug of the current, an echo bounced from mountain walls after a whistle cord was pulled, and the sound of water rushing over rapids.

One young pilot used these skills during a run from The Dalles to Upper Cascades (near the town of Stevenson) on a snowy November night in 1876. The *Daisy Ainsworth,* one of the most luxurious sternwheelers on the mid-Columbia, was substituted for a smaller boat to carry a large herd of beef cattle. When a short distance from his destination, and with only a narrow chute between rocks and shore to navigate through, the pilot guided on the only light visible—it turned out to be that of a waiting train. The wharf light had been blown out by the wind; the *Daisy Ainsworth* crashed on the rocks. The pilot and crew were saved, but many cattle were lost. The pilot died a few months later—some said of tuberculosis, others said of a broken heart.

The town of Stevenson sits on low bluffs, its residential area spreading across rolling hills. For a long time it was known to all rivermen as Shepard's Point. George Stevenson bought part of Shepard's claim in 1893 and laid out the town. A dock stands on the waterfront.

*The old locks at Cascade Locks*

You may tie up for a brief or overnight stay and walk into town for supplies. Stay clear, however, of the space used by the sternwheeler *Columbia Gorge*. It stops here three times a day from June to September.

The community of Cascade Locks, built on a shelf alongside the river beneath massive, towering mountains, is one of the oldest in the gorge. It started in 1853 when three white families settled here, with Indians as neighbors. Here a series of rapids fell steeply for 2½ miles, and the lower rapids cascaded to tidewater. For years this presented the last dangerous river passage for explorers and settlers. Indian trails were initially followed around the rapids, then commercial portages were built—first a wagon road, then a railroad.

Later, steamboats carried passengers between this portage and the one above The Dalles. Boats built on the mid-Columbia were sent to Portland when they were no longer needed, and had to run the rapids at high water. The *Hassalo* shot the rapids in May 1888, its hull creaking and heaving as it rushed through white water at one mile a minute. Once it was down, it could never return.

The locks around the upper rapids were completed in 1893. Dur-

*The Columbia Gorge is rapidly becoming one of the world's
hot spots for wind surfing*

ing their construction, workers lived in tents and shacks, and the population of the town swelled to one thousand. Portions of the walls and stonemasonry of the old locks can still be seen, and are the focal point of a beautiful waterfront park and museum.

In the center of spacious green lawns stands the first locomotive used on the portage railroad. This engine, called "the Oregon Pony," was also the first locomotive to operate in Oregon.

During the summer, the sternwheeler *Columbia Gorge* is berthed at Cascade Locks. This replica of early-day sternwheelers that plied the Columbia sails three times a day for two-hour excursions with boardings at Stevenson, Bonneville Dam, and Cascade Locks. In the winter it is berthed in Portland and sails excursions on the Willamette River.

The marina is located on the up river side of the park. Moorage and gas are available. A large building overlooking the river houses the port office, a museum, restrooms, and showers. Downtown is a short walk through the park and under a railroad bridge. The main street parallels the river and is attractively lined with restaurants, motels, and stores.

Be sure to visit the museum before you leave Cascade Locks. Displays there will take you back to the times when the portage railroad carried freight and passengers around the rapids, when crews built the locks, and steamboats raced to be first through the locks.

# Cruise
# Seven

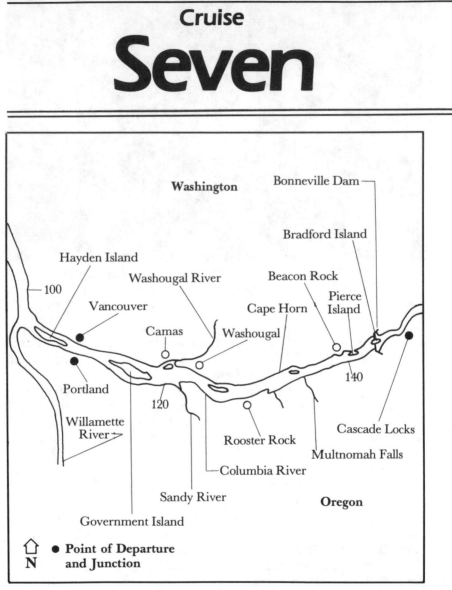

Washington

Bonneville Dam

Bradford Island

Hayden Island

Washougal River

Beacon Rock

Pierce Island

— 100

Vancouver

Cape Horn

Camas

Washougal

Portland

140

Willamette River →

Cascade Locks

120

Rooster Rock

Multnomah Falls

Columbia River

Sandy River

Oregon

Government Island

⌂
N

● Point of Departure
   and Junction

*Do not use for navigation.*
*Use NOAA Nautical Charts 18526 and 18531*

# Cascade Locks to Portland and Vancouver

**Point of departure:** Cascade Locks, Oregon

**Course:** Columbia River via Lake Bonneville and Bonneville Lock and Dam, with a vertical drop of 64 feet to tidewater

**Stops:** Beacon Rock State Park, Rooster Rock State Park, Reed Island, Port of Camas-Washougal, Government Island, Portland marinas

**Length of cruise:** approximately 40 statute miles

**Duration on power:** 1 day

**Duration on sail:** 1 to 2 days

**Overnight moorage:** Beacon Rock State Park, Port of Camas-Washougal, Portland marinas

**Junction point for Cruise Eight:** Portland, Oregon; Vancouver, Washington

# Top of Tidewater

Tidewater lies ahead. Tidal influences reach inland up the Columbia to the bottom of Bonneville Lock and Dam, a little more than three miles downstream from Cascade Locks. Even before Bonneville was built, this was the upper reach of tidewater, since the ebbs and floods were stopped by rapids. The upper and most dangerous rapids were opposite the town of Cascade Locks. They were called Hi-Yo-Skookum Chuck ("very strong water") by the Indians, "the Great Rapids of the Columbia" by Lewis and Clark, and later, Cascades.

Though you follow the river's course through the top of tidewater for part of this cruise, you are still in the Columbia Gorge and move beneath its high, timbered mountains and the waterfalls pitching over their slopes. The gorge ends near the Sandy River delta, and from there it is only a few miles downstream to the outskirts of Portland and Vancouver. The tidal influence on this cruise is about a one-foot change.

As you leave Cascade Locks, you swing past all that remains of another Memaloose, or Indian burial, island. It was once known as Sullivan Island, and covered twenty-five acres, but only its top has shown since the lake waters rose. It is located close to shore, and the odor sometimes became too much for the early settlers who lived nearby. One night in 1855, some of the men rowed out to the island and set it on fire.

The first portage around the rapids was built in 1851 on the north bank. One mule pulled one car over the two-mile wooden tramway that rounded river bluffs and crossed gullies on wooden trestles.

In March 1856, Indians attacked the settlers on the north and south banks of the rapids. Some of the besieged remained for three days in a blockhouse and the Bradford Store on the north bank near the present site of the Bridge of the Gods. The battle ended when military units arrived from Fort Vancouver, but not before several settlers and Indians had been killed and many wounded.

The narrow river ahead is spanned by the Bridge of the Gods. Today it is a fine tracery of forged steel, but in Indian legends it was a bridge of stone. One legend tells of a wise old Indian woman who guarded the bridge. Despite her faithfulness to her post, the bridge collapsed when the peaks now known as Mount Adams and Mount Hood (Indian gods) fought for the affection of Squaw Mountain. They spat ashes and fire and hurled white-hot rocks that struck the bridge. The fighting continued, the earth shook, and the bridge and the old woman fell into the river. The Great Spirit, who was grateful for the old woman's faithfulness in guarding the bridge, said he would grant her one wish. Because she was old and ugly, she asked to be beautiful and young. The Great Spirit granted her wish—she became Mount Saint Helens. In light of the 1980 eruption, the legend now has an interesting twist.

One scientific hypothesis of the stone bridge's origin is that thousands of years ago a mountain slide from the Oregon side blocked the river, causing it to back up and form a huge lake. Later erosion may have then produced the natural stone Bridge of the Gods.

The river, squeezed on the northern edge by a slide that occurred seven hundred years ago and by high banks on the south, is narrow through this stretch to Bonneville Dam. The waters are deep and there is a set to the current, so keep a firm grip on the wheel or tiller.

Along the banks a few wooden platforms hang out over the water. These are used by Indians who fish with dip nets as their ancestors did for thousands of years.

At Eagle Creek, on the south shore above Bradford Island, small craft can take refuge from winds. Do not use the inlet, however, if the creek is flowing fast during a seasonal freshet.

Bradford Island was named for two brothers, who were early settlers in this area. The island is composed of layers of silt called the Eagle Creek Formation, which is visible as you pass by. It is part of an ancient riverbed that predates the Cascade Mountains. Though barely visible from the water, a remnant of more recent times can be seen on the upper end of the island. A gray, moss-covered "pillbox" still stands there as it did during World War II when it guarded Bonneville Dam.

Bonneville Lock and Dam is split by the island. The spillway is on the north side, the locks and powerhouse on the south. A second powerhouse to the north was completed in 1981. These two powerhouses are the oldest and newest federal power plants on the Columbia.

A dock juts into the lake on the south side of the island above the powerhouse, and during the summer permits access to the visitors' center. The dock, provided by the Port of Cascade Locks, is used for boarding passengers on the sternwheeler *Columbia Gorge*. Although the Port wants the public to use it, there are some minor restrictions. The tour boat arrives at the dock at 10:00 A.M. and 12:30 and 3:00 P.M., and needs the up river side for loading and unloading its passengers. They are dockside for fifteen minutes. Should you want to use the dock, tie to the down river side or wait until the tour boat is gone.

*Sternwheeler* Columbia Gorge

The visitors' center at Bonneville is worth a stop. Here you can observe migrating fish at eye-level through a viewing window, see displays that show how the dam operates and from an observation deck take in a broad view of the dam and its setting.

When you approach the dock you are above the powerhouse, so watch for a faster-moving current and its pull in this area. If you decide not to stop at the visitors' center, the best approach to the lock is to stay to the Oregon shore.

This lock is the oldest, the smallest, and the last of the locks on the inland waterway. With this last stair-step drop of sixty-four feet, you will be at sea level but still 145 miles from the ocean. Because of the lock's small size, tugs that moved through other locks comfortably have to break up their load here and make up to five lockages before continuing down river. Another user of the locks, one not visible from the surface of the water, is the local fish population. It was recently discovered that smelt, sturgeon, and anadromous fish "locked-through" instead of using fish ladders for migration upstream.

Bonneville's second powerhouse was built to harness the power from surplus water passed over the spillway. To make way for the powerhouse, a highway, railroad tracks, and town were moved. The town of North Bonneville, Washington, population about 600, was relocated to the west.

While construction progressed, archeologists worked at an ancient Indian village site downstream from the powerhouse. They found thousands of artifacts ranging from centuries-old tools and pottery to whiskey bottles and buttons from the mid-1800s. They also uncovered large house pits believed to be ones described by Lewis and Clark on their descent of the Columbia in 1805.

Just below Bonneville, your navigation skill may be put to the test dodging boats on a weekend or a holiday. This area is considered one of the best spots to fish for sturgeon, and on such days numerous small boats fill these waters.

In earlier days, the shores were lined with about twenty huge fishwheels scooping up salmon from the west end of Bradford Island to Beacon Rock. Salmon caught in the wheels above the cannery at Warrendale were stuffed in kegs and floated down river. Portable wheels suspended on scows also worked these waters. The wheel could be moved up and down. In the down position, it picked up fish and dumped them in the scow. When the scow was loaded, the wheel was pulled up. One wheel got stuck in the down position and kept turning, dumping salmon on the scow until it sank.

On your trip thus far, human intervention in the form of dams has changed the geography, obliterating pieces of history. The passing years have not changed this part of the river, however, and from here on down it remains much the same as when explorers first found it. This provides a pleasant feeling for boaters. You find you become more at one with what you glide by. You muse about how it appeared to Lieutenant Broughton, to Lewis and Clark, and to the many families who used this river as the main street of their lives.

Though the river seems broad about two miles below the dam, the channel itself is narrow. Off the main channel, water covers shoals and shallows. One such area is around Ives and Pierce islands, near the north shore above Beacon Rock and about four miles below Bonneville. Beacon Rock, a plug-shaped monolith, is the throat of an ancient volcano: it rises nine hundred feet above the water and stands as a prominent, well-known landmark in the Columbia Gorge. It is reportedly the second largest rock in the world, after the Rock of Gibraltar. Seen from the distance, the scrub trees growing in patchy soil and the striations of weathered rock create a rough, broken surface. The marine park at the rock's base is a favorite spot for Portland and Vancouver boaters who are out for a day or a week. This is a recommended stop for a swim, lunch, an overnight stay, or just a closer look.

Enter on the downriver side of Pierce Island. The docks, located in an inlet below Beacon Rock, are sturdy and wide, and comfortably accommodate foot traffic from tie-ups on both sides. At the top of the ramp in a wooded area, a parking spot and grass spread around a small bluff. The bluff drops toward the river to a creek that flows into the inlet. The park also has a launch ramp and picnic tables. Since this is a long hike from Skamania, the closest town, groceries and gas are not available, but some boaters hike up a trail through the woods to a tavern on the highway.

*Fish boat at Cape Horn*

Generally, waters in the lower Columbia are cool for swimming. Here in the inlet the waters are warmer, however, and those who would not swim elsewhere have enjoyed a plunge here. To combine sand, sun, and swimming, row to the east side of Pierce Island where you'll find a beach with sand to run your toes through.

If you pulled in early in the evening, you may not have seen the railroad track that curves around the top of the inlet. In the middle of the night your sleep may be broken by a sudden roar and a piercing oscillating light—it may seem as if the train is racing headlong into the dock.

A trail up to the top of Beacon Rock is safe and easy, requiring only endurance. Once at the top, you'll feel it was worth the climb for the view of the Columbia Gorge.

Beacon Rock's history is as interesting as its geological features. More than eighty years ago, the Army Corps of Engineers planned to dynamite the rock for use in a breakwater at the Columbia's mouth. Railroad officials sued and stopped the blasting, since they did not want the rubble on the track. In 1915 Henry Biddle bought Beacon Rock and spent $10,000 to build a trail to the top. When Biddle died, his heirs offered it to the State of Washington for $1 if the state would turn it into a park. When Washington refused, the heirs offered it to Oregon. Oregon accepted, but before Oregon proceeded to build an Oregon state park in Washington, Washington officials changed their minds and finally bought Beacon Rock for $1.

As you untie to move down river, others will be readying to go up river. Beacon Rock is the "cracker-barrel country store" for boaters. Everyone stops here, so it's a great place to pick up the latest tidbits of cruising lore as well as meet and vacation with landborne travelers.

Across the river at Warrendale there is a boat launch and dock, and another dock down river at Skamania, Washington.

The height and precipitous pitch of the mountains on the Oregon side for the next few miles are reflected in the white, feathery lines of falls streaking down through green forests.

Horsetail Falls is just down river past Saint Peter's Dome, a rounded column rising three thousand feet. About three miles farther down, Multnomah Falls, the best-known falls in the gorge, drop in a stair-step of 620 feet. A visitor's lodge built in 1925 is located at the bottom.

Wahkeena Falls (its name comes from the Indian word meaning "most beautiful") and Mist Falls are just down river from Multnomah Falls. Mist Falls leaps into space from a twelve-hundred-foot cliff and turns to spray.

While watching the falls as you move down river, also keep an eye on the chart. Just before Multnomah Falls, the channel begins to angle across the river through a narrow slot between Fashion Reef on the Oregon side and an island edged with sandy shoals. When strong winter easterlies blow, tugboat captains moving barges down river wait before proceeding around Fashion Reef. With the high-sided barges acting like sails, the captains fear the easterlies will push them aground on the reef.

The channel swings to the Washington shore and follows it a short distance to Cape Horn, a sheer-sided headland dropping straight into the water. Winds blowing from the east and the west sometimes meet head-on at this point.

Summer winds below Bonneville, in the reach of the river, covered by this cruise, are not as strong or gusty as they are through the middle and upper parts of the gorge. A skipper who has spent several summers sailing the waters between Bonneville and Portland told us that though it may not be as windy as up river, strong winds can come up suddenly.

It was a submerged rock rather than winds that caused a sinking near Cape Horn over a century ago. The James P. Flint, the first steamboat constructed in the mid-Columbia, was being moved to Portland because of a lack of passengers and freight. During the run it safely negotiated the swift water over Cascade rapids, but it struck a rock in quiet waters at Cape Horn and sank.

The large rock off Cape Horn is a remnant of an old landslide and is called Phoca Rock. *Phoca vitulina* is the generic name for the harbor seals who swam here in the early days. Stay between it and Cape Horn.

The channel angles back across to the Oregon side to Rooster Rock State Park. The park runs along the shore east of Rooster Rock, another monolith like Beacon Rock but smaller. Large parking lots and picnic grounds are shaded by old, tall cottonwoods. In the summer, the park is a popular gathering place for boaters, picnickers, and nude sun-bathers. At the base of Rooster Rock, water from the river fills a small, shallow lagoon where there is a launch ramp.

On the hill above the park stands Crown Point, a favorite viewing and picture-taking spot on the Columbia Gorge for those traveling in cars. The highway curving by the point is the old Columbia River Scenic Highway, and from the river you see snatches of its stonework among the trees and over the draws. Called a "cornice" because it clings to cliffs, its design originated from the old techniques used in Germany. Two and a half miles of the roadway are anchored to cliffs by dry masonry work.

Just downstream is Corbett, Oregon. This marks the farthest point up river that Lieutenant Broughton reached in 1792.

The tree-covered island across from Corbett is Reed Island. In the winter, the hardwoods appear as bunches of bare ming trees but are

*Crown Point at the Columbia River Gorge*

soft and green in the summer. Reed and two other islands, Flag and Gary, southwest of Reed in the curve of the river, are favorite mooring places, although in recent years, Gary and Flag have been used less due to silting.

The upper end of Reed is shallow, and depths are affected by tide and release from Bonneville. A group of twenty-five boaters unaware of these depth changes anchored near the upriver side of the island; the next morning all were high and dry.

The waters that are safe for anchoring and near a beach are on the north side of Reed. Follow the river as it swings north toward Washington, and come in from the west side.

In this swing to the north, the river flows around Oregon's Sandy River delta—the largest delta in the Columbia River—and into a broad valley. The steep sides of the gorge now taper down into low hills. With this change in the topography, one can understand why many consider the Sandy River to be the western boundary of the Columbia Gorge. The Sandy was named Quicksand River by Lewis and Clark after they left their canoes to wade across the delta and sank in the sand.

In the spring, smelt swim up the Sandy while hundreds of gulls swoop overhead, then dip to catch the silvery morsels. Indians also caught the oil-rich smelt, but used them for candles rather than food.

As the river swings north, then west at Camas-Washougal, it enters the eastern outskirts of the Portland-Vancouver area. The islands and open waters between the two cities have become a favorite boating area for city residents. As one boater put it, on race day on a summer Sunday, "the river is wall-to-wall boats."

These upstream waters are used more than those downstream of the metropolitan area. The nearby islands are one reason. Another is the river's current. Many skippers, especially owners of boats with displacement hulls, like to start a cruise going against the current, then return running with the current.

From Camas-Washougal to Portland and Vancouver, where the Interstate 5 bridge connects the latter two cities about fifteen miles downstream, there are numerous possibilities for places to stop for an overnight. You may choose to anchor at an island, then pick up gas and supplies the next day at a marina. Or you can tie up at a marina, or at one of the docks at the three Thunderbird Motels clustered around the interstate bridge, leaving your boat to enjoy dinner or a night on shore in a bed that doesn't rock. A few of these will be described in detail below.

The towns of Camas and Washougal, sometimes referred to as the Gateway to the Columbia Gorge, are separate but close neighbors. Washougal (the name is derived from an Indian word meaning "rushing water") lies to the east, where a branch of the Pendleton Woolen Mills is located. The Washougal River, which comes down from the northeast near the town, was first named Seal River by Lewis and Clark, who found many seals living on rocks along the river.

In Camas, a city that has been making paper since 1884, the main industry is Crown Zellerbach's specialty paper mill. The name Camas originates from a lily that Hudson's Bay Company fur trappers called "La Camas."

Several explorers—including Lieutenant Broughton, who visited the Indians here—were surprised to find a white man with red hair living among them as their chief. He was called Chief Soto. The story written in journals tells of a young Spanish boy on a ship with his father when the ship sank near the mouth of the Columbia, most of the survivors were massacred by Indians, but the boy was spared and raised by the Indians.

The first settler in Washougal, David Parker, built a log cabin in 1845 at the place later called Parker's Landing. Today, the Parker House stands on the landing and is a favorite Sunday brunch site for boaters from Portland. The restaurant, overlooking the marina at the Port of Camas-Washougal, also serves lunch and dinner. Boats are permanently moored here, and there is a guest dock as well as a pump for gas and diesel. If no one is at the pump, ask for assistance at the port office.

In front of Camas-Washougal, stay in the marked channel. There are shoals and reefs on either side; some are exposed. Marker number fifty sits on a pebble shoal. "Ough" Reef to the north is named after a person, but when we first saw it and the name, we thought it had been named for the exclamation of a boater who ran into it.

The river angles southwest past Lady Island, once the site of an ancient Indian village. Excavations have revealed that it was the oldest site of continuous occupation in the lower Columbia. It dates back to 400 B.C.

The channel continues southwest then turns northwest between Government Island and an island to the north. During high water, the current is swift through here. The north island, although unnamed on the chart, is called both Sand Island and Steak Island by local boaters, and is another favorite boaters' spot. Someone has surmised that the name Steak Island originated because of all the steaks cooked there on summer evenings. There is a good anchorage between the island and the Washington shore. Because of shoaling between the tips of Lady and Steak islands, the safest approach is from the western end. Once at the end, however, do not short-cut it close to the island, you may go aground. This holds true for many islands in the lower Columbia. Submerged shoals build and shift on both ends of the islands, so the safest approach to any island is always to give its ends a wide berth.

On the north shore of Steak Island, you can drop the hook and dinghy to the beach.

Just below Steak Island, Gentry's Landing on the mainland is an easily accessible fuel stop. Log rafts once stored at Government Island directly across from Gentry's were considered a hazard to navigation, so they have been removed, and the State of Oregon has built a dock there for pleasure boats. It provides access to the island and can be used for overnights.

Even though you are drawing close to the metropolitan area, you will still feel some distance away. Except for a new highway bridge ahead, there is little yet to indicate that the cities exist. On the mainland, large homes are set back among the trees, with lawns reaching gracefully down to the river's edge. One home stood in the path of the engineer's ruler, and bridge piers now stand in its sideyard.

At the west end of Government Island are Sand and Lemon islands, the latter another favorite of boaters. Because its banks drop away quickly, some boaters put the bow on the beach and drop a stern anchor.

The origins of the names Government and Lemon reach back into history, but those like Steak Island and Beer Can Alley, an inlet on Government Island, are of more recent origin. We have never sailed into Beer Can Alley, but it is not hard to imagine how it got its name.

Lieutenant Broughton and his expedition pulled past Government Island without recognizing it as an island. Lewis and Clark named it Diamond Island. It was called Miller's Island when the government took it over in 1850 for military purposes and for raising hay. The name Government has been with the island ever since.

As you round the end of these islands there is little doubt that you are boating through the largest metropolitan area on the inland waterway. On the Washington side, more homes and more buildings crowd in above the shores and on the hills east of Vancouver. Large jets feather down at Portland International Airport across from the islands.

Marinas stretch along the Oregon shore to the interstate bridge, several of them with fuel and overnight moorage. Watch for the colorful oil company emblems that indicate gas docks. If they do not take overnights, they can point the direction to a dock that does.

Hayden Bay, rimmed with condominiums on the upriver and north side of Hayden Island, has dock facilities and is a short walk to a Safeway market. The three Thunderbird Motels mentioned earlier are just down river, clustering around the interstate bridge. Two are on the north side of Hayden. The Red Lion stands east of the bridge, the Jantzen Beach to the west. Across the river is the Inn at the Quay in Vancouver.

If you are in a mood to enjoy shoreside pleasures, try one of these docks and motels. The two on the Oregon side of the river are within easy strolling distance of the Jantzen Beach Mall, replete with movie theaters and shops. Two have special appeal to boaters: the Recreational Equipment (REI) store, and a well-equipped boating store, Cal Marine. Safeway is also within walking distance from here.

On Cruise Eight, you will sail quickly out of the metropolitan area into a rural setting only a few miles from Portland and Vancouver. On the river ahead, there are interesting sights, whether you are just leaving Portland for a weekend getaway or continuing on a longer cruise.

# Cruise
# Eight

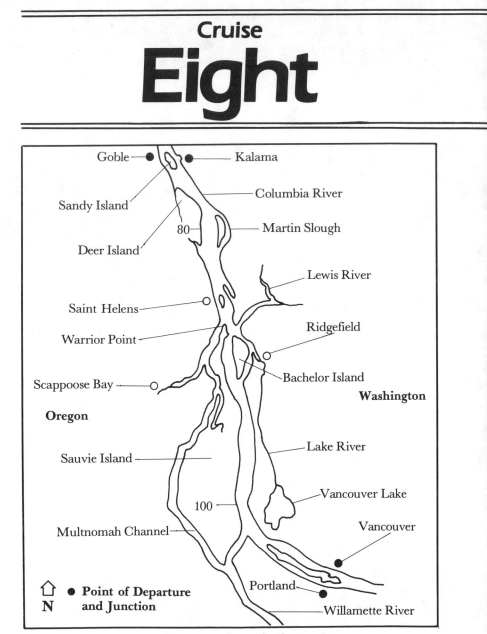

Goble ● ● Kalama

Columbia River

Sandy Island

Martin Slough

80

Deer Island

Lewis River

Saint Helens

Ridgefield

Warrior Point

Bachelor Island

Scappoose Bay

**Washington**

**Oregon**

Lake River

Sauvie Island

Vancouver Lake

100

Vancouver

Multnomah Channel

Portland

● **Point of Departure**
**N** **and Junction**

Willamette River

*Do not use for navigation.*
*Use NOAA Nautical Chart 18524*

# Portland and Vancouver to Goble and Kalama

**Point of departure:** Portland, Oregon; Vancouver, Washington

**Course:** Columbia River main channel, or via Willamette River and Multnomah Channel

**Stops:** Main channel route: Leeward Isle Marina, Ridgefield, Saint Helens, Martin Slough, Sandy Island, Goble, Kalama; Multnomah Channel: Brown's Landing, Coon Island Marine Park, Scappoose Bay

**Length of cruise:** approximately 30 statute miles via the main channel or 40 statute miles via Multnomah Channel

**Duration on power:** 1 day

**Duration on sail:** 1 to 2 days

**Overnight moorage:** Main channel route: Leeward Isle Marina, Ridgefield, Saint Helens, Martin Slough, Sandy Island, Goble, Kalama; Multnomah Channel: Coon Island Marine Park, Scappoose Bay

**Junction point for Cruise Nine:** Goble, Oregon; Kalama, Washington

# Weekend Getaway

One advantage of living in the Pacific Northwest is that the edges of the "outdoors" are woven into the fringes of the cities, so you don't have to go far to leave the metropolitan atmosphere behind. Boating on the Columbia River is no exception. For a weekend getaway from the Portland and Vancouver area, you can head up river, stopping at some of the coves and beaches mentioned in Cruise Seven, or you can head down river.

Cruise Eight follows the Columbia on its last northward stretch as it parallels the Cascade Range before turning west and pushing through the Coast Range. Heading either up or down river, you quickly glide into the quiet countryside.

If you need to launch a boat, Portland and Vancouver have several launching areas with ramps. Some public and private ones are on the Columbia along Marine Drive in Portland. In Vancouver, a ramp is located in a small park above the interstate bridge and the Columbia Industrial Park.

Through warm summer evenings and weekends, and on brisk winter Sundays, the area from Government Island to the interstate bridge fills with racing sailboats and powerboats slicing through the water. Almost a century and a half ago, this part of the river was dominated by Vancouver, not Portland. Indian canoes and fur traders' bateaus plied these waters toward the Hudson's Bay Company's Fort Vancouver. For nearly twenty years, beginning in 1825, this fort was the trading and cultural center of the Pacific Northwest. Located on grounds just east of the bridge, a restored stockade and the buildings it surrounds are hidden from the river view by a dike.

The Hudson's Bay Company, in early control of the western fur trade, moved its headquarters from Astoria in 1824, about twenty years before the first settlers arrived in Portland. Under the direction of Chief Factor, or manager, Dr. John McLoughlin, the fort was referred to by one traveler as a "New York of the Pacific."

Men, such as mountain man and explorer Jedediah Smith, who the night before had eaten around campfires, pulled themselves up to a table set with Spode china, Waterford glass, and sterling silver. They ate lamb, pork, sturgeon, or salmon smothered in butter and cream sauces, all accompanied by imported wines. For dessert, they were served fresh fruits and cheese.

Large vegetable gardens and orchards grew outside the stockade. Inside stood about forty buildings, including a pharmacy, warehouse, stores, living quarters, and a building that served as a church on Sundays and a school the rest of the week.

Contrary to Hudson's Bay Company policy, McLoughlin aided many immigrants who arrived over the Oregon Trail. When the United States was awarded jurisdiction of the Oregon Territory, the Hudson's Bay Company moved its headquarters to Victoria, British Columbia. The U.S. Army later built barracks and officers' quarters around the fort. From the river, these buildings can be seen standing on a knoll among trees west of the stockade.

A first lieutenant was stationed at Fort Vancouver as Quartermaster in 1852—his name was U.S. Grant. He tried several schemes to earn extra money to bring his family west, but they all failed. He shipped ice to San Francisco, but the market melted before the ice arrived. He shipped chickens; they died en route. He planted potatoes, but they were flooded.

To cruise through these two metropolitan areas, you may want to go south of Hayden Island through North Portland Harbor. On this waterway the interstate bridge has a vertical clearance of thirty-four feet, and the railroad bridge downstream clears thirty-nine feet. Many permanent moorages, houseboats, and a container dock at the west end line the shores of this narrow channel.

Following the main channel of the Columbia River along Vancouver, you will pass beneath the interstate bridge, where the clatter of cars speeding across fills your ears as you approach its double green span. Because of the current's push, steer clear of the bridge pilings.

During World War II, Liberty Ships were built on the now empty ways at the Columbia Industrial Park. This and the Port of Vancouver cover most of Vancouver's waterfront east and west of the bridge. Ships tied here, their mooring lines scaled to their large size, take on grain and lumber and unload steel, automobiles, and chemicals. Like David meeting Goliath, you feel minute as you pass by the huge hulls, some freshly painted, others rusted by years at sea. Painted beneath the overhangs on the docks in difficult-to-reach spots are names of seamen and ships from foreign ports.

A short distance downstream from the interstate bridge, a railroad bridge crosses the river. If you want the swing span on the Washington side opened, give the signal: one long blast followed by one short.

Below the bridge you enter the fringe area—not quite city and not quite "outdoors." On the Washington side, the port and its buildings give way to trees along the shore. At the confluence of the Willamette and the Columbia just ahead stands Kelley Point. The trees and sandy beaches of a hundred-acre park on the point are bounded by the activity at the Port of Portland.

This area is also the upper limit for ocean freighters moving into the Port of Vancouver, North Portland Harbor, and up the Willamette River to Portland. Even though at times this can be a busy intersection for freighter and tug traffic, it offers no problem if skippers observe the rules of the road. Accompanied by whistle signals and churning prop wash, ships back out of berths at Terminal Six just above Kelley Point. Near Vancouver, they sometimes lie at anchor, so watch for their anchor chains.

The park at the point has been set aside as a natural area. In the summer its beaches are crowded with picnickers and swimmers, while boaters launch their boats at a nearby ramp. If you plan to put in here, watch for the wake of passing ships.

For many years this point had no name. In 1792, Lieutenant Broughton named a point in this vicinity, Belle Vue, and some historians feel it may have been this one. A later traveler coming the full length of the Columbia in a rowboat in 1925 claimed he saw five mountain peaks from here—Jefferson, Hood, Adams, Saint Helens, and Rainier.

The southern tip of Sauvie Island lies across the Willamette from Kelley Point. This low island filled with lakes and marshes is about 15 miles long and 4½ wide, and is the largest island in the Columbia River. Its presence offers two courses to the boater: one continues down the main channel to the east of the island; the other, Multnomah Channel, flows along the west side of Sauvie, shadowed by high green bluffs on the Oregon mainland. The two merge near Saint Helens, Oregon.

To reach Multnomah Channel, turn up the Willamette River for a short distance. The channel begins just before reaching high overhead power cables near Fred's Marina. If you need food or fuel before starting, both are available here.

Portland's industry seeps into the upper parts of the channel, but you quickly leave it behind to move along a narrow waterway that meanders between the dikes on the island and the tree-scattered shores of the mainland. On this nineteen-mile stretch you will pass architecturally fascinating houseboat communities, skirt a gamebird watcher's paradise, ease past log rafts, move over for tugs, and pop into small marinas. You can spend the day circling the island and then return to Portland, or you can end the day in a tucked-away bay or at Saint Helens, replete with small town accoutrements. Because of the relative narrowness of the channel, most sailboaters go under power rather than sail. However, it is possible to sail if the winds are right.

With little gas in the tank, one skipper had to sail up the channel.

*Float houses on Multnomah Channel*

As the boat moved silently over water the color of milky tea, he looked up to see a deer swimming the channel ahead of the boat.

Sauvie Island was once home to a large tribe known later as the Multnomahs. Their largest village was located along the Columbia near the upriver end of the island, and is now partially under water. Lewis and Clark named the island Wap-pa-to referring to the wapato root, a staple of the Indians' diet. These explorers traded trinkets for the root, which Clark described as being "equal to the Irish potatoe, and . . . a tolerable substitute for bread." The present name of the island comes from Laurent Sauve, a French-Canadian who operated a dairy on the island for the Hudson's Bay Company.

If the dikes were gone you would see a landscape little changed since the Indians lived here. The famous Sauvie oaks were growing when Columbus sailed the seas.

Like most early pockets of civilization, Sauvie boasted a fort, Fort Williams, at the downriver end of the island. About a mile below the bridge that connects the island to the mainland stands the only restored vestige of those early days—the Bybee-Howell House built in 1856. To see it, tie to a log raft and row the dinghy to the dike. Following the road on the other side, enjoy the easy walk to the house, which is an example of the nineteenth-century territorial farm life. An orchard of century-old cherry and pear trees is in the yard behind the house. The house is open daily during the summer months. Check the hours; they change annually. If you are a late fall cruiser, don't miss the unique celebration called "Wintering In," held the last Saturday of September. At this time, orchardists and produce-growers bring in their best for sampling and judging.

Even with the dikes, the wild fowl are fascinating. Much of the island is a state waterfowl management area. During the summer months you can see great blue herons, killdeers, sandpipers, and snipes on the shore and turkey vultures, red-tailed hawks, doves, and pigeons in the air. In the winter months the swans gather. A local wildlife agent commented, "You know, some people think there aren't many swans around. Why, heck, we've got over three thousand right here in the last part of December."

While the island has an abundance of history and wildlife, the channel is teeming with waterborne people. The houseboat communities show how seriously the residents take their waters: more and more are choosing to live not just near them but on them. The individualistic architectural styles of these homes are bound to fascinate the photographer, artist, or casual observer. Ingenuity abounds: at Brown's Landing, wedged in between other craft, is a partially transformed trimaran, with the beginnings of a house taking shape around its bows.

Heed a note of warning concerning the wake problem for these water-dwellers. Posted speeds are strictly enforced. Skippers running boats with deep V-hulls also need to be aware that, when slowed down, such hulls create a much larger wake than expected. It is better to stop completely, then ease into gear gradually. This will stop the sucking action of the water and lessen the wake.

A variety of moorages dots the channel. Many have only houseboats and offer no services to boaters. Brown's Landing, about nine miles down the channel, does have both houseboat moorage and dockside service. It also has a few extra spaces and can take boats up to twenty feet long overnight. There is no electricity or water, but gas and diesel are available as well as ice, beer, wine, and some food. Quiet and safe, it is open from 8:00 A.M. to 6:00 P.M. Closed Mondays. Brown's also rents canoes, which reflects a fast-growing craze on the channel. Members of the Lower Columbia Canoe Club canoe here. One good trip of about nine miles takes four to five hours, including a lunch stop. It moves from the channel up the Gilbert River on Sauvie Island. Following a course through lakes and sloughs, with only short portages at some times of the year, it has become a favorite "splash and glide" trip.

Fishing year-round in this area is also popular. Depending on the season, fishermen bobbing about in boats gather on Multnomah Channel, the Columbia, or nearby tributaries. One local marina owner summed up the fishing year. "In January sturgeon starts getting hot and a few winter steelhead are left. In February sturgeon stays good, the first spring Chinook begin to show, and dippers begin to get smelt on the Lewis River." By mid-April spring Chinook peak. "Lots of 'em.

We see between forty and sixty per day." In early summer shad come in. By August, "There's fall Chinook in Lewis River, also steelhead. There's some excellent fishing." A few Chinook linger through November. In December, "sturgeon fishing starts improving."

If you want a break from fishing or an overnight stop, there is Coon Island Marine Park three miles below Brown's Landing. It has picnic facilities and three hundred feet of dock space.

At the entrance to Gilbert River, about two miles below Coon Island, there is a launching ramp and moorage on the island side. Boats can cruise up Gilbert River (which may be the shortest river in Oregon). Take note of tides, however, before entering. As one local laughingly noted, "Oh, I've seen them stuck there high and dry. . . and for some time, too. Guess they don't realize we still have tidal action here, from two to three feet."

One note of caution: island ownership is either private or state game refuge land. This eliminates places to pull a runabout on shore. You can, however, tie up to log rafts for a lunch break, a swim on a hot summer day, or an overnight stop. Should you tie up for the night, select deep water between the log raft and shore. One night before realizing the problem of wakes from other boats, we tied to a raft on the channel side and leapt from bed several times during the night to fend our boat off the log raft.

For a quieter night's rest, check your charts for the entrance to calm Scappoose Bay. The Bayport Marina is about 1½ miles in from Multnomah Channel. In the 1800s, this quiet and secure moorage was a winter haven for sailing ships. Watch the entrance carefully, and as you go in, stay to starboard of the numbered markers. Dredging is done only within this channel, so not even one foot outside it is safe. Do not be misled by the open expanses of water luring you away: those are muddy Sirens in disguise.

Scappoose Bay offers excellent fishing for bass, catfish, shad, and sturgeon most of the year. The Bayport Marina has overnight moorage. There is a good launching ramp, and sailboats with four-foot draft can be hauled out—mast down, as there are wires over the ramps. Gas is available, and although no diesel is offered at the dock, a diesel truck can make a run out from Saint Helens if enough volume is needed. Restrooms and picnic areas are avilable. Come in July and you'll have a good chance of sharing in the Christmas-in-July celebration with the Hayden Island Yacht Club.

This quiet, secure moorage can be a pleasant stop on a pleasure cruise. If someone in your party is a member of the Moose, you can enjoy an evening at their club, including a restaurant and dance floor, directly across the road from the marina.

The bay is a dead end, so you retrace your careful steps before you continue downstream.

Near the end of Multnomah Channel on Sauvie Island are the remains of a large boatyard. Except for the piling, little of these extensive old wooden ways is now visible.

From here you may want to head to Saint Helens, which is just to port. Or swing around the tip of the island and around Warrior Point, point the bow up river, and you will be headed to Portland and Vancouver.

To cruise the Columbia below Kelley Point, continue down the main channel, leaving the freighter docks and shipping cranes behind. The river is wide as the bow follows a sun-scored path on the water. Pass the mouth of the Willamette and you move into a rural setting edged by low sandy beaches. On Sauvie Island, a few riverside dwellings stand among the trees. On the Washington shore dairy herds graze near barns, and in the distance is the collapsed gray top of Mount Saint Helens. For several miles down river you will have good views of this active volcano.

The beach at Hewlett Point, Washington, looks quiet now, but in the winter of 1980 pieces of a nine-year-old mystery were found here. Picnickers pushing sand aside for a firepit discovered decayed clumps of $20 bills. Two days later, crowds of FBI agents descended on the spot and began sifting through the sand. The money was later identified as part of the $200,000 that hijacker "D.B. Cooper" carried with him when he bailed out of a Boeing 727 over southwest Washington on 24 November 1971. No trace of "Cooper" has been found.

A short distance beyond Hewlett Point, the Leeward Isle Marina is tucked behind Caterpillar Island. The entrance is directly across from marker number twenty-eight. From the river, the sandy shores and scrubby trees on either side of the entrance seem to blend together, and it is difficult to spot the first time if you are going fast. The marina has overnight berths, diesel, gas, water, and ice, and takes boats up to sixty-five feet long. In addition, they do inboard and outboard repairs and have a hoist.

Just below marker number twenty-eight, the Marshall Beach Tavern, a gray building with portholes and a sign, sits atop a wide sandy beach. This is the only restaurant on Sauvie Island. Skippers in runabouts frequently beach their boats to stop for a beer, pizza, or hot dogs. Several "no's" are posted on a sign near the tavern. One reads, "No nude sunbathing." Away from crowds and under sunny skies, these bare sun worshippers proliferate, particularly near the downriver end of Sauvie Island.

The mild, rainy climate of the lower Columbia River Valley and the marshes, myriad sloughs, and shallow lakes that extend beyond the river's edge offer compatible habitat for migrating birds. Some of these areas have been set aside as refuges. From marker number seventeen to the entrance to Bachelor Island Slough the shoreline is part of the western boundaries of the Ridgefield Wildlife Refuge. Many birds winter here, and deer, coyote, fox, raccoon, and beaver live here year-round.

Near the end of Bachelor Island, opposite the black channel marker, clusters of nests made of rocks and sticks fill the treetops. This is the largest great blue heron rookery in the Pacific Northwest. In the springtime, when the cottonwoods are leafed out, the five hundred nests with the young are obscured, but you may see adults flapping about as they leave or return to their nests.

Bachelor Island, where geese and ducks winter, has cultivated fields of grain and potatoes. The potatoes are grown for the Frito-Lay Company to use in making potato chips. The island was so named because three bachelors were the first to settle on it in 1849. They rowed across the river each day to work at a mill in Saint Helens.

The upriver entrance to Bachelor Island Slough is passable during high water. Sailboaters should be cautious, however, about traveling this slough during spring high water. Power lines cross the slough (marked on the chart), and one sailboat was dismasted when it hit a line.

Warrior Rock Light, a white pyramid structure, stands downstream a short distance offshore from Sauvie Island. Warrior Point and Warrior Rock are well known on the river for both peaceful and tragic events. In 1792, Lieutenant Broughton found his boat surrounded by

*Warrior Rock Light on Sauvie Island*

canoes carrying Indians wearing war garments. He made peace with the Indians, but left the name, Warrior.

Mariners have had difficulty in this area, especially in adverse weather. Ships have gone aground, one as recently as 1984; others have collided and sunk. One foggy winter evening in 1898, the sternwheeler *George W. Shaver* collided with a larger sternwheeler, the *T. J. Potter*. The *Shaver* was a magnificent ship. It was famed for its delicious food prepared by Chinese cooks, and for its size, which accommodated three decks. Freight traveled on the lower deck, the pilothouse sat on the top, and passengers lounged on the middle deck. When the *Shaver* sank in eighteen feet of water eight minutes after the collision, gossip was thick with accusations that she was deliberately rammed to eliminate hot riverboat competition.

Directly across from Warrior Rock Light, two rivers flow from low banks and merge with the Columbia. Beyond the banks and several miles distant, high hills rise abruptly. The Lewis River to port is navigable for sailboats about one and a half miles upstream to the fixed railroad bridge. In early spring, hundreds of gulls wheel and dive as they follow the smelt run up the Lewis.

Lake River to starboard is navigable upstream for about three miles just beyond the historic town of Ridgefield, with a city dock and gas available at a marina. This river also serves as the outlet for Bachelor Island Slough.

During fishing season, the waters near the mouths of these rivers and at Warrior Point are dotted with fishermen in "kicker boats." During duck season, small boats scoot in and out of Lake River going to and from hunting expeditions. To enter Lake River, work the tides. Shoaling occurs near the mouth, and there are plans to dredge it to ten feet. The depths inside are good. For a short distance, the river runs between the mainland and Bachelor Island.

Should you sail up this hundred-foot-wide channel at particular times, especially in the spring, you may be surprised—the river flows backward. Vancouver Lake, where Lake River heads, is lower than the Columbia River. During spring runoff, when the Columbia River is high, the backward flow sends large volumes of water from the Columbia up Lake River to Vancouver Lake. During the summer, when the river is low, water flows from Lake River into the Columbia.

High, grassy banks on Bachelor Island slope down into the river. Along the mainland shore cottonwoods and willows lean over, some dipping into the water. This tree-covered shoreline—where deer can be seen occasionally—forms another boundary of the Ridgefield Wildlife Refuge.

Passing the junction of Bachelor Island Slough and Lake River you see millworks rising above the trees. Beyond the mill are a small

*Heron rookery on Bachelor Island*

city dock, a launching ramp, and the Ridgefield marina, where houseboats and boats are berthed. Gas and water are available at the marina but not transient moorage. You can, however, tie up at the city dock. From there it is just a short walk into this quiet town for hamburgers or supplies.

If you decide to save Lake River for another day, Saint Helens, Oregon, lies ahead beyond Warrior Point. This historic, picturesque river town was founded as a village in 1845, and for many years in the late 1800s and early 1900s it was a center for logging and shipping. Vestiges of the old mixed with the new can be seen as you approach the town. Poised on a bank above the river, the old gray courthouse, built of stone from a nearby quarry, with a white cupola perched atop a broad roof, stands next to the new courthouse, its stark lines formed by brick and glass. The old courthouse is still in use, and houses a small but attractive historical museum.

There are two moorages at Saint Helens. One of them, the city dock in front of the courthouses, is free. It is not well protected, and afternoon winds and wake from other boats are a problem. The other, just down river, is Saint Helens Marina, a full-service marina, open year-round. They have transient moorage, gas, ice, and a ramp. This is also a good spot to obtain fishing information and supplies.

Though they are exposed to the wind, some boaters tie to rafts—when the rafts are there—at Sand Island in front of Saint Helens. Improvements have been made on the island. It is now Sand Island Marine Park, one of the few marine parks on the Columbia. You can tie up to the docks, enjoy a picnic, or relax on the beaches. Yet this island, where trees grow and deer roam, retains its natural character.

The old part of Saint Helens is a short walk up from the waterfront. Although many businesses have relocated inland, nearer the highway, you will find a small grocery store near the courthouse. Two blocks away is the Saint Helens Cafe, which offers one of the best breakfasts on the river. You know there must be a steady breakfast trade to justify its 5:00 A.M. opening. For late night entertainment, the Bar Harbor Restaurant adjacent to the courthouse offers a lounge and service past midnight. A worthwhile stop in town is the museum in the old courthouse. The past and present are so tied together in this building that you must be careful to find the right door on the second floor, and not end up in a current court session in the next room.

The town originally known as Wyeths Rock, then Plymouth, and finally Saint Helens because of its proximity to the mountain, was, in its early days, in competition with the small town of Milton on Scappoose Bay. Town promoters were busy then offering two free lots to each married man and one lot to any single man who would build a house and make Milton his home. But Milton is gone, and Saint Helens survived.

Its early history was fast and furious. Logs and sawmills and the people and machines working with them powered her into the 1900s, when good logs in the water sold for $3.50 to $4.00 per thousand feet. Modern sawmills and a pulp mill operate here today.

Rock quarries also added to the prosperity. Beginning in 1895, rock was extracted from quarries for twenty years. In 1909, over three hundred men were employed in the industry.

It was shipbuilding that really brought fame to this town. When the days of sailing ships were coming to a close, the marine architects found it difficult to abandon them altogether: three motor ships were built, but they carried sails. As late as 1915, the *Wapama*—a wooden-hulled, oil-burning lumber schooner—was christened here. Until 1947 it bore lumber cargoes and passengers up and down the Pacific Coast. Now it is moored at the Maritime Museum in San Francisco Bay.

Hills and mountains have been with you as you have been following the Columbia from Portland and Vancouver, but always as a distant backdrop. As you cruise by Saint Helens, however, timbered slopes with squared patches of clear-cuts move closer to the river on the Oregon side. This is the eastern edge of the Coast Range. In Washington, these mountains begin their rise from the valley west of Woodland. As you follow the course that the river has taken to breach the Coast Range, bluffs crowd close to the river along some stretches, then give way to deltas and valleys along others.

Just below Saint Helens is Columbia City where old and new homes mingle above the water's edge. Although there is no moorage here now, at one time it, too, was a thriving port and busy boatbuilding site. The boatyards, the last operating as late as the 1940s, built large wooden vessels.

One winter morning we motored below this area. Fog hung about us, and ice still clung to the deck. About midday the fog withdrew, revealing a view of three major mountain peaks—Saint Helens, Adams, and Hood. Against the sharp blue sky they stood out like white paper cut-outs. Despite the cold, fishermen and beachcombers walked the low, sandy bluff on the Washington shore.

This was the scene we saw and wrote about prior to the Mount Saint Helens eruption on 18 May 1980. Writing about the mountain then, it was hard to avoid the usual clichés written about majestic mountains. There are no clichés to describe now the catastrophic event that tore off the top of the mountain.

A small bay on Deer Island, directly across from Martin's Island, provides a safe moorage. Freighter traffic turns in the channel here, where the river swings slightly in a westerly direction, and the swells go outside the bay. The dock and all land are privately owned, so anchoring out is the only possibility.

The stacks beyond Deer Island belong to Reichhold Chemical. In 1979 the company drilled for gas near Mist, located in the Coast Range, and discovered the first commercial supplies of natural gas in Oregon. The gas now provides some of the power for the plant, as well as heat for homes in Portland.

On the Washington side a slough that runs around the back edge of Martin Island is an active log raft area. It is sometimes a bit too crowded for easy boat maneuvering as tugs move in and out, leaving and hooking up to rafts. Nevertheless, its deep, protected waters make it an active tie-up area for pleasure boats. A thin stand of trees grows between the highway and the slough and offers a buffer to the sounds of passing cars and trains.

Some distance down river, massive concrete structures stand in stark contrast to the trees and bluffs nearby. The closest, grain elevators at the Port of Kalama, are about two miles away. Beyond them another four miles, on the Oregon shore where the river disappears around a bend, stands the cooling tower of the Trojan Nuclear Plant.

Below the grain elevators, the river splits as it flows around Sandy Island, with the main channel staying to the east side past Kalama. In this vicinity, several choices are possible for an overnight stay. Along the waterway between the island and Oregon, you can anchor or tie to log rafts. Or you can tie up at the docks at Goble, Oregon, or at the marina in Kalama, Washington.

Because of shallows at Hunter Bar near the upper end of Sandy Island, stay mid-channel if you sail to the west of the island.

At Goble boaters can pull into Scipio's Goble Landing. The backdrop of trees and hills makes for a pleasant stop. Here you will find moorage, gas, water, showers, and boat ramp. If you want to stretch your legs, or need ice, food, or sundries, a quick jog across the railroad tracks will take you to downtown Goble, which has one service station, a store complex, and a tavern. The store has gas, wine, ice, quick sandwiches, and basic groceries. It is open from about 6:30 A.M. to 8:00 P.M. The tavern has great hamburgers and entertainment.

Goble is a prime example of a town whose past size and glory are lost in the dust and sawdust of time. Few now know of her former fame, but she was once a southern terminal of the huge rail ferry *Tacoma,* which carried up to thirty-two cars at a time. In 1908, completion of a railroad bridge at Portland brought an end to this ferry service from Kalama.

Across the river on the Washington side, the Port of Kalama Marina offers more facilities for stops. Approaching the marina from up river you see the town rising steeply on the hillside. A small white Catholic church built in 1909 and now a state historical landmark and a few historic homes, survivors of early fires, stand out among the newer homes.

The marina, protected by a large jetty and barely visible from the water, lies at the foot of town. Its entrance is at the lower end of the jetty. Watch for four large totem poles standing in the city marine park. These were carved by Chief Don Lelooska about twenty years ago, and have been repainted several times by school children. The tallest totem, measuring 150 feet, was carved from a single log. For many years the totems stood near the Columbia Inn in downtown Kalama, then were moved to the park. Chief Lelooska, working vigorously to keep Indian legends and dances from fading into the past, conducts living history programs in his hometown of Ariel, Washington.

The port office sits on the jetty beyond the totems, and beyond that is the entrance. It is well marked, and a large sign inside points the way to guest moorage. Diesel, gas, water, electricity, pump-outs, and a launch ramp are available. If there is time before dusk, you may want to walk into town for supplies, for a meal at one of the restaurants, or for a closer look at the historic Catholic church. It stands on the site of a church built in the late 1800s, at a time when Kalama expected to be a boom town.

In 1870 the Northern Pacific Railway planned its transcontinental terminus here. The town was suddenly gorged with laborers who had money to spend and entrepreneurs who had schemes to reap that money. Lots were subdivided, and when the flat land was gone, they moved up the hillside. In this "high times" atmosphere, someone dreamed up the motto, "Where rail meets sail." It is still used today. In 1873, when the railroad was completed between Kalama and Tacoma, the Northern Pacific moved its western headquarters to Tacoma. The boom slowed, and later a fire burned ninety percent of the town.

The first settler in Kalama was Ezra Meeker, who built a cabin near the mouth of the Kalama River in 1853. He is best remembered because he came west from Ohio by wagon and returned when he was ninety-four by plane.

A large cannery once operated in Kalama, and its pilings can still be seen near marker number forty-nine. Chinese worked in this cannery, as they did in so many of the canneries on the Columbia. In recent times the sands near the pilings have yielded many Chinese coins, some minted in brass with a square hole in the center.

At rest now and secure for the evening, you have many miles of this river trip behind you. This stretch of the Columbia becomes a pleasant recollection, and maybe one that will entice you to future weekend getaways. As you've seen, there are many places to explore and stop each time.

The next segment offers entrance into what is known as the lower Columbia, and also what we have called volcano country. Traveling the river you are always at a safe distance from Mount Saint Helens. Thus far, you've seen the mountain, but on the next cruise you will see evidence in and along the river of the flooding caused by its 1980 eruption.

# Cruise
# Nine

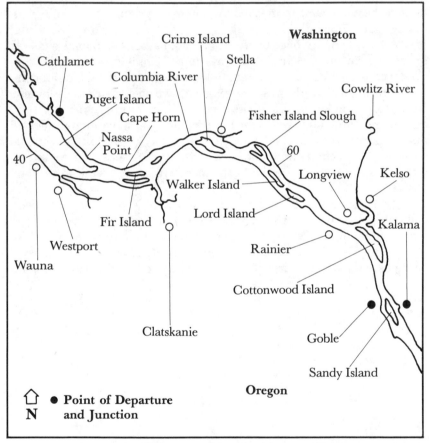

Washington

Crims Island

Stella

Cathlamet

Columbia River

Cowlitz River

Puget Island

Cape Horn

Fisher Island Slough

Nassa
Point

60

40

Walker Island

Longview

Kelso

Fir Island

Lord Island

Kalama

Westport

Rainier

Wauna

Cottonwood Island

Clatskanie

Goble

Sandy Island

Oregon

⌂  ● **Point of Departure**
**N**      **and Junction**

*Do not use for navigation.*
*Use NOAA Nautical Charts 18524 and 18523*

# Kalama and Goble
# to Cathlamet

**Point of departure:** Kalama, Washington, or Goble, Oregon

**Course:** Columbia main channel along south side of Puget Island and back to Cathlamet; alternatively, Columbia main channel and along north side of Puget Island down Cathlamet Channel to Cathlamet

**Stops:** Rainier, Walker Island, Fisher Island Slough, Clatskanie, Westport, Elochoman Slough Marina

**Length of cruise:** approximately 40 statute miles via south side of Puget Island and 35 miles via north side of Puget Island

**Duration on power:** 1 day

**Duration on sail:** 1 to 2 days

**Overnight moorage:** Rainier, Walker Island, Fisher Island Slough, Clatskanie, Elochoman Slough Marina

**Junction point for Cruises Ten and Eleven:** Cathlamet, Washington

# Volcano Country

From Kalama to Astoria the river continues to spread outward. It strays from its main channel and ambles behind and around islands into shallows and narrow sloughs, eventually forming a broad estuary below Skamokawa. This area is considered the lower Columbia region.

On 18 May 1980, part of this area felt the impact of the eruption of Mount Saint Helens. This cruise takes you past the mouth of the Cowlitz River, where millions of cubic yards of mud and debris plunged into the Columbia following the eruption. Evidence of this now appears in a narrower shipping channel and new land developed from the dredge spoils. The Columbia and its banks upstream and downstream from the Cowlitz have been changed, yet the character of the lower Columbia region remains intact.

Except for Longview and Kelso, population in the green valleys and timbered hills in this region has decreased in recent years. The area is sparsely settled; some call it "primitive." When the river was the only highway, fishing, logging and sawmilling were the main industries. Most are now gone, but the remnants of weathered gray shacks and broken pilings that supported a cannery or sawmill stand along the shore.

Beyond the river, hills and ridges covered with stands of hemlock and fir and a ground cover of fern, salal, and huckleberry are evidence of heavy rainfall. At Naselle, Washington, a short distance inland from the Astoria bridge, the annual rainfall is over one hundred inches. In the early 1900s, this climate and the fishing appealed to many Finns and Norwegians. They settled the area by clearing or diking the fertile bottomland for farming. Even today their descendants, like those on Puget Island, practice the folk art and traditions of their ancestors.

You will seldom see clusters of powerboats and bare masts here, except on holidays. Then, coves and the few marinas fill up with boaters from Vancouver and Portland. To escape the crowds, daring skippers try a sport called "gunk holing." Exploring sloughs slowly and watching depths, they look for quiet hideaways.

Although this cruise can be covered unhurriedly in a day, you may want to push off early, since summertime westerlies frequently begin to riffle the water soon after breakfast or by mid-morning. They continue to blow and gather strength, pushing the water into scattered whitecaps. When these winds blow, they are often as steady as those striking across San Francisco Bay. These are good conditions for sailing, but they create an uncomfortable ride for small powerboats. You may also choose an early departure to stop for a walking tour of a historic town, or to drop the hook for a picnic on a sandy beach.

As you leave Kalama or Goble, the dominant feature on the Oregon shore is the cooling tower of the Trojan Nuclear Plant. Interestingly, its billow of steam floating skyward is not always an indicator of the winds at river level. The cloud may drift straight up while brisk winds blow on the river below.

Follow the main channel past the end of Sandy Island and between the cooling tower and the green marker. North of the marker the Kalama River flows into the Columbia, mounding sand into shoals. Unwary sailors at the helm of boats with fixed keels often go aground here.

The day is warming. On the Oregon shore sunbathers spread their towels and blankets. Across the river, cows graze in the shade of trees or stand knee-deep in the river. By noon, crowds gather on the eastern end of Cottonwood Island. This is known locally as a good place for picnics and water-skiing, especially in the protected waters of Carroll's Channel.

With skiers and ski-boats to dodge, you may wish to avoid this channel during the day. At night, however, when everyone has gone, there are good moorages alongside log rafts on the Washington shore. Tall cottonwoods muffle the sounds of traffic on the highway, but not the occasional loud splash in the water. You turn quickly, hoping to see a large salmon jump, and discover a beaver slapping its paddle-tail on the water.

As the main channel bends around the bluffs across from Cottonwood Island, the smokestacks of Longview's industrial area come into view, and you move into the area affected by the volcano.

On the downriver end of Cottonwood Island, the Cowlitz merges with the Columbia. The surge of the mud and debris caused filling in of the Columbia upstream from the Cowlitz as well as downstream. It is estimated that five to ten million cubic yards, which is a normal year's dredging for the entire Columbia, was dumped. Millions of board feet of logs floated in the river as salvage operations began and some logs were picked up miles below in the estuary. Salmon migrating up the Cowlitz leaped out of the heated water and became stranded on debris.

Until dredging of a new shipping channel was begun, large freighters could not traverse the area, and those already in Portland and Vancouver were locked in up river for a couple of weeks. The Cowlitz was also severely affected.

Once, the river was navigable several miles upstream, but what was then a leisurely cruise is no longer possible, since the river was mudded in and its depth of ten feet reduced to three. Ramps and moorages also filled with mud. Although dredging was done and check dams were built on the tributaries, authorities feel the Cowlitz will continue to fill during the rainy season with runoff from the Mountain's denuded flanks. The situation could keep changing in the years to come, and you should seek out local information if you plan to go outside the main channel of the Columbia along this stretch.

Fishermen used to congregate around the mouth and along the shores of the Cowlitz to catch salmon, steelhead, and smelt. Weeks after the eruption, some fish were observed trying to make their way up river.

The docks and cranes protruding from the shore ahead are part of Longview's waterfront. Sometimes the river is crowded as freighters lie at anchor in the channel waiting for space to take on cargoes. The city lies on the broad, open flats beyond, its business section some distance from the waterfront. Unlike most communities along the Columbia, Longview was built after roads began to thread their way along the river's banks, so residents did not need to rely on the river for their transportation.

Longview, a planned city, sprang up from the flats in 1923, many years after its neighbor, Kelso, started near the banks of the Cowlitz. Because the area was filled with marshes and lakes, miles of diking were built first. The intricate dikes and pumping stations were patterned after those in the Netherlands. Some of the land within the city lies at the same elevation as you do, bobbing about on the river. This allows Longview residents the unique experience of looking out a window on the flats and seeing what appears to be an ocean liner flowing gracefully through the fields, the top of the stacks floating above the dikes.

The surrounding area with its timber potential was acquired to support the grand plans of R.A. Long in his design of the perfect city. The design followed the "spoked wheel" configuration similar to that used for Washington, D.C., and some European cities. Streets radiate out from the hub, the center of town. Since then, the city's population has grown to more than 30,000 and spreads beyond the wheel.

Although there are no docks or moorage for pleasure boats in Longview, a short tack across the Columbia takes you to Rainier, Oregon, and moorage there.

When the town was founded in 1851, it was named Eminence, but by 1852 the name was changed to Rainier. Once a steamboat landing, Rainier remains a traditional port town, with small wooden homes and churches extending in neat rows from the base of the harbor to the crest of the hills. In the late 1800s, sturgeon were the major source of income.

Later, they would appear on restaurant menus as "river bass."

Another claim to fame was lost when this little town ceased production of Rainier Soap. In the early 1900s this soap, sold in a wrapper carrying a picture of Mount Rainier, was billed as "Nature's Own Preparation." It was a best-seller. Made of lye from nearby hills, it had a long list of allegedly effective uses: it was an antiseptic; it was good for skin diseases; it prevented blood poisoning; it removed spots, grease, and stains; and it cleaned woodwork. A true product of nature, it also claimed to be free of chemicals and dirty fats.

Today, local businesses have redone the older port. Here boaters are greeted by the Rainier Marina where there is a sandy playgound that provides swings and slides for children and a public restroom.

The essentials of food and drink are within easy reach in this town. A regular grocery store is nearby and an excellent natural foods store is two blocks around the corner. The liquor store is in the small drugstore on the corner down the street.

For seventy-two years prior to Longview's founding, Rainier dominated this stretch of river. Its shoreline provided good docking for steamboats. Shores across the river were marshy. Passengers and freight headed for Puget Sound would transfer here to boats of the Cowlitz Canoe and Bauteau Company to take a thirty-four-mile—two-day—ride up the Cowlitz River. A remnant of Rainier's steamboat era—the 1888 House—stands west of town. This fourteen-room house was build by George Moeck for his wife and six children. Moeck ran a general store and dock where river captains stopped for supplies.

If the short break turns into an overnight, note that the moorage is affected by the wake of passing freighter traffic. Using an inside berth will ensure a less bumpy night. Gas and ice are available, and although the dock area is not enormous, it can usually handle most traffic stopping for the night.

There are few gas docks from here on down river. The only ones are at the Longview Yacht Club (for yacht club members with reciprocals) on Fisher Island Slough; the Kerry West Marina at Westport, Oregon; and at Cathlamet, Washington, before heading out across the Columbia estuary. Diesel is available at the marina in Cathlamet. There are no signs on the Columbia advising boaters about where the next fill-up is possible.

When you do cast off, food and fuel well in hand, swing out into the main channel of the Columbia, and you will begin to pass one of the new land areas built with past eruption dredge spoils. It extends from Rainier to the Lewis and Clark Bridge. The bridge's name is new, but the bridge is over fifty years old. With a clearance of 195 feet and a central span of 1,200 feet, it was once the largest spanned cantilever bridge, and the highest over navigable waters.

On the north is Weyerhaeuser Company's log-booming and rafting grounds, followed down river by its pulp and paper mills. Next look for the mounds of white salt at the site of the chlorine plant. For millions of years a magnificent formation, Mount Coffin, stood on the same spot. Lewis and Clark stopped here briefly in November 1805, and described Mount Coffin: "A remarkable knob rises from the water's edge to the height of 80 feet, being 200 paces round the base." It served as an early navigational marker for mariners and a burial place for the Indians, and was also known as Memaloose Ilahee. In 1908, Mount Coffin was sold for $10,000 as a rock quarry. Many tried to save it, but the knob soon disappeared.

Even though marine parks are scarce on the lower Columbia River, many islands invite boaters to come ashore. Some have clearings where you can pitch a tent. Most have tall cottonwoods and alder, and a variety of wildlife on or near the islands. Canada geese have been observed on Lord and Walker islands, the two islands just down river on the Oregon side. These islands are rimmed with sandy beaches on the north shore and log rafts on the south. Behind Walker Island there is a beautiful cove where you can tie up for the night. Steep cliffs crowd in from the mainland on one side, and the tree-covered island hides river traffic on the other. Off the main channel and near the upper end, you are protected from the wake of passing ships. Here it is quiet, and warm wood smells drift up from the log rafts. The only disturbance might be the freight train making its nightly run to Astoria on the tracks that skirt the foot of the steep cliffs.

At one time the Oregon State Marine Board considered buying hundred-acre Walker Island to develop a marine park, but because the board was unable to find local government sponsors, the project was dropped. A favorite with boaters, it is owned by Knappton Towboat Company.

The entrance to Fisher Island Slough is across from Walker Island. Moorage along the diked mainland is home for the Longview Yacht Club and a growing houseboat community. Like barnacles, the dwellings are encrusting each piece of shore. Limited guest moorage is available by the clubhouse, a white float house displaying the club insignia. The gas dock is just up from the clubhouse.

Fishing the Columbia, whether from a boat or with a line cast from the shore, is a favorite sport regardless of the weather. As protection from the elements, innovative shore fishermen gather driftwood and plastic sheets to fashion makeshift fishing shacks. These squat along the shores near and below Fisher Island, the island south of the slough, as well as on other beaches. Setting their poles outside in the fog or rain, the fishermen gather around a fire inside. From the river, these

*Moored to log rafts near Walker Island*

shacks look like hobo town. When winter winds blow, most lie tumbled and forgotten. Some are rebuilt the next season.

Below Fisher Island the river opens into a large basin where, bounded on the north and south by cliffs and mountains, it swings around Crims Island. Near Mayger, Oregon, a weathered boat and net-house hang over the river, supported by tall pilings. Just west on

Crims, brightly colored tents sometimes are scattered like confetti beneath the trees. We cruised this way one summer day. With the heat and the sun's glare flashing from the water's rippled surface, it was difficult to imagine that during severe winters years ago, the river was frozen from shore to shore. When it was, children who lived at nearby farms tied on ice skates and skimmed across the frozen river.

Three white buildings with red roofs are all that remain of the early town of Stella, Washington, across from Crims at the mouth of Coal Creek Slough. In its heyday during the early 1900s, Stella was the center of more logging activity and camps than anywhere else on the river. Today, the neat buildings look out of place among the river's natural, weather-battered structures. At one time they were part of a community that included two hotels, Brock's General Store, and a blacksmith's shop. Stella was named, it is said, for the hometown of a German itinerant preacher who came from Portland to serve the people here.

Arriving by boat, you are entering Stella's back door, as these buildings now face the highway that parallels the river. Such would not have been the case in 1902, when the river was the focus of all these towns. Today, the remaining homes and businesses, with backs to the river and the past, welcome their trade from the road and its endless stream of car travelers.

Stella has a singular claim to fame related to the early logging business: here Simon Benson invented his famous "cigar rafts." Needing a way to transport large quantities of logs to San Diego, California, Benson designed a raft that was capable of carrying three million board feet at one time; the resulting shape resembled a huge cigar. The rafts proved seaworthy, and reached San Diego in twenty days.

Today the Old Stella Tavern makes an interesting afternoon break. But watch the entrance to the bay at Coal Creek Slough. It is shoaly at the mouth, but there are good depths inside. A word of caution when investigating here and elsewhere in the lower Columbia: if you have a choice, always investigate on an incoming tide. Should you go aground, the rising water will lift you off. There are some pilings and a ramp of sorts at the rear of the tavern. It is risky for larger boats, and a short move down Coal Creek Slough provides a much safer tie-up at a float. Then a short walk back to the tavern is a good prelude for a quaff on the back porch of the tavern. Neither groceries nor gas is available at this spot.

Crims Island was first named Fanny's Island by Lewis and Clark for Clark's sister. Although the island's name changed, the upper end is presently called "Fanny's Bottom." A small cove between Gull and Crims islands on the downriver side is at the outlet of a narrow waterway that disappears into the trees. If you want to go up this waterway, cross the inlet at high tide, for shoaling occurs here. If it is low tide and you are looking for a place to tie up, there are log rafts tied in Bradbury Slough on the southwest side of Crims. Follow the mainland shore of the slough before crossing over to them. Although the rafts provide secure moorage, the area is open and not protected from westerlies that sweep across the broad, diked farmland. When we tied here, we grabbed towels and walked across the logs until we found a swimming hole between the logs and the shore. The plunge into the water felt refreshing on that hot day. Waters in the lower Columbia tend to be quite brisk for many swimmers, but if you find a shallow beach or a back eddy where the water moves slowly and is warmed by the sun, swimming can be very enjoyable.

Abernathy Creek, across the river on the Washington side, is quiet now, but before white men moved west, an Indian village stood along the banks of the creek and river. Later, a large sawmill buzzed with activity as each year millions of board feet of logs were cut into lumber. Now only broken pilings are left.

Logs to this mill moved down from the hills on trains and by means of splash dams. Invented in 1881, these dams were used to transform quiet streams into torrents. Logs were dumped behind dams built across a creek, then when the dams were choked with water and logs, all were released to crash downstream.

The dock and oil storage tanks just down from Bradbury Slough is Port Westward, the site of Portland General Electric's turbine plant.

Along this narrower portion of the river, with high bluffs on the Washington side and open fields on the Oregon side, winds are not always steady or predictable, and small whirlpools swirl at the base of the bluffs near the riprap that supports the highway. These conditions do not present a problem to pleasure boaters.

A few years ago, however, a miscalculation here became a problem for the captain of a navy tender—his ship plowed into the highway. At the repair dock, yellow paint from the highway's center line had to be scraped from the bow. It is said the slogan of the ship became, "Sighted highway, sank same."

Down river at Eagle Cliff, trees hide any traces of Hume's Cannery, built in 1865, or the docking area for steamboats. Across the river, Fir Island has sandy beaches and warmer water for swimming.

When meandering tributaries of the Columbia are navigable, they often offer interesting side trips that penetrate the land beyond the river. One such trip follows Beaver Slough and the Clatskanie River up to Clatskanie, Oregon. The mouth of the slough is on the upstream side of Wallace Island. Depending on your idea of a full cruising day, the speed of your boat, and the whims of the second mate, this trip can take all day or a leisurely afternoon, or become an overnight excursion. It is also a great introduction to slough navigation. As you enter the slough, those leggy net sheds to your left are like many you will see in this area.

Slough navigation can be classic here. Following what appears to be the main channel, you may wind up instead at a dead end or at an abandoned sawmill. Use the chart, for it is a reliable guide. The waterway is diked and marked with remnants of fish-receiving stations, some still in partial use. Behind the dikes you will see an occasional cow or silo in flat fields. You are now traveling a back alley once used as a main highway.

The railroad drawbridge over the Clatskanie River remains open except when a train passes over. Then the tender cranks the bridge closed and then open again by hand. For twenty-five years Jess Guidry operated the bridge over the Clatskanie and lived in a small house next to the bridge until he retired in 1981. Drawbridges over Blind Slough and the John Day River operate the same way.

Just up around the bend from the bridge, you'll find both the end of navigational waters and a good moorage dock at Hump's Restaurant. Although neither electricity nor water is available, the docks provide plenty of space and overnights are possible.

Whatever your plans for the night, take the time to eat and go sightseeing. The dining room overlooks the river, and you'll eat on the exact spot where, in the 1800s, you might have booked passage on a steamboat—$0.50 deck, $1.50 first class with a meal. A lounge with a postage-stamp dance floor and nightly live entertainment can spice up the evening.

To walk off the meal, visit "The Castle," a short distance up the hill. This home with twin turrets was built in 1900 and is in the National Register of Historic Places. It is open for tours.

When you return down the slough to the main channel of the Columbia, the safest route is the way you came in. After leaving Beaver Slough, the open waterways are tempting shortcuts, but they hide many shallows.

Cape Horn, a headland down river from Eagle Cliff, rounds out into the river. Like those around its namesake, the waters below it are often choppy, as the wind gusts in from the west. Beyond Cape Horn, Puget Island acts as a wedge splitting the river into two routes to Cathlamet. The most direct one flows between Puget Island and the Washington bluffs. The longer one follows the main channel on the south side of the island. Should you choose the more direct route, swing out from Cape Horn to avoid the chop, then move in toward the rock riprap below the highway.

Just before Nassa Point, move out and toward Puget Island. An old motel, its gas pumps boarded up, stands across the highway at

Nassa Point. Water in this area is shallow, and sailboats often go aground if care is not taken. Because of shifting river silt, a good route one season may be too shallow the next.

Before crossing back from Puget Island to follow the mainland cliffs, check the chart and watch the depth finder. Exercise care and you will not be confronted with problems.

If you are spring cruising, move close to the bluffs so you can see the colorful, varied wildflowers. Some are tucked into rock grottoes splashed by a wispy waterfall. A few madrona trees grow along the bluffs, but this is about the last location you will see them. Local residents and river people say these trees will not grow farther down river because the climate is too wet. Beyond the bluffs the Puget Island bridge crosses the channel; its span is sufficiently high for sailboats to sail under. Cathlamet lies just down river.

Taking the longer cruise around Puget Island, you will see more farms and houses, some new, some old, but most built by Norwegians and their descendants. First a gravel bed, the island grew with the continuous deposit of silt. Indians at one time lived here in lodges built on poles to protect themselves from the freshets and high tides. Lieutenant Broughton named the island for one of his men, Lieutenant Peter Puget. It was not until the dikes were built in the early 1900s that permanent settlement took place. When Norwegians caught "American fever," many came straight from Norway to Puget Island.

In places the island is eight feet below highwater level. It covers four thousand acres, and nearly seven hundred people (about fifty more than in Cathlamet) call Puget Island home. Their crafts are a way of life: if a fisherman needs a boat, he builds it; if a woman needs lace for trim on a dress, she makes it. Many still observe Scandinavian holidays such as Norwegian Independence Day.

Westport Slough is soon to port. Each day, every hour between 7:00 A.M. and 5:00 P.M., a small ferry—the last one on the lower Columbia—sails from Puget Island up this slough to a landing near Westport. Between the bridges at Longview and Astoria the ferry is the only connecting link for nonboaters along a sixty-mile stretch between Washington and Oregon.

Just beyond the ferry dock is a small moorage with floats. There are two eating establishments a short walk up Toll-Ferry Road. The Plympton Creek Inn serves homemade soups and sandwiches. The King Salmon Lodge, set among trees where a creek runs, serves lunches Tuesday through Friday, Friday and Saturday dinners with reservation by calling (503) 455-2400, and Sunday brunch.

Farther up the slough is Kerry West Marina, where gas, marine supplies, and moorage are available.

Across from Wauna, where Crown Zellerbach's pulp mill stands, is

*Church on Welcome Slough*

the entrance to Welcome Slough. This is one of eight Puget Island sloughs used by fishermen in the late 1800s. Here their boats and nets could lie quietly in the water away from the swift river currents. The slough, open to small sail and powerboats, takes you into the heart of the island, past farmland and grazing dairy herds. Homes and a church still face the waterway.

As you follow the main channel around the west end of Puget Island, you will see high bluffs now on the Oregon side. An open sweep of water, then lowlands extending to rolling hills mark the Washington side. The bluffs may look solid, but here, as in other sections of the lower Columbia regions, unpredictable landslides occur. Many years ago, in the middle of the night, a slide plunged into the river creating a wave that swept across the channel and washed two homes off the top of the Puget Island dike.

The meadows on your right once bore the heavy hoofprints of draft horses pulling in dripping seine nets of salmon. Remnants of old horse barns can still be seen on neighboring Tenasillahe Island.

Off the lower end of Puget Island is Blue Heron Island, unnamed on the chart but known locally by this name because of a great blue heron rookery there. The nests, about a hundred in all, are visible in the winter, when the leaves are off the trees. Because the great blue heron is seen most frequently as a solitary, aloof water bird, the sight of large groupings is surprising. The call of the hungry chicks in early spring assaults the ear, when the multitude sounds in unison.

You are now in sight of Cathlamet, with its homes and churches perched on a riverside knoll. Shallow shortcuts here may put you aground. Go beyond Blue Heron Island, then up mid-channel to Cathlamet.

You can pick up supplies in two places in Cathlamet: a dock on the waterfront or a protected boat basin, which also has overnight moorage. The dock is west of the Puget Island bridge at the River Rat Tavern float. It is a three-block walk to the main street and a grocery store. The boat basin, Elochoman Slough Marina on Elochoman Slough, is west of the tavern's dock.

Whether approaching the entrance to the slough from east or west, stay between the green marker and the sign "100 feet of Boat Basin." On the downriver side of the marker, the entrance is silted in.

Overnight moorage, water, gas and diesel are available in this harbor, which is cupped among trees below a hill to the north. If you need gas to continue on to Astoria, arrive before 5:00 P.M., when the marina employees go home. Unless you have seen the town before, however, Cathlamet is well worth a long stop because of its museum and historic buildings.

Cathlamet is the county seat of Wahkiakum County, the smallest county in the state. One of the first river towns in the lower Columbia region, Cathlamet was started in 1846 by a former employee of the Hudson's Bay Company. An Indian village stood west of town where the Crown Zellerbach Company buildings now stand. When Lewis and Clark were here in 1805, they saw a strange sight: burial canoes placed high in cottonwoods, with their prows pointed to the west.

*Cathlamet waterfront*

When an Indian died, he was wrapped in robes and furs and placed in his canoe with paddles to await "the flood of life" to come in like the tide. Many were still in the trees when the first settlers arrived.

Today some of the older buildings have been restored, and a walk into town takes you back in time. Cathlamet, like Skamokawa down river, retains a flavor of its historic past. One of the oldest houses in the state stands on Main Street and is still occupied. Built in 1857, when Washington was a territory, the house was designed and constructed by James Birnie, the town's founder. Down along the waterfront on Commercial Street, you can see the oldest remaining cannery on the Columbia. This one, the Warren Salmon Cannery, was built in 1869. Chinese worked here until the late 1930s. Today it is used as a net shed.

Now comfortably moored, before turning out the lamp you may want to check the chart to help you decide on tomorrow's cruise through the Columbia River estuary. There are three courses you can take to cruise the estuary. The most direct one follows the main shipping channel to Astoria, Oregon, and across the Columbia River Bar. Or you may choose Cruise Ten or Eleven; each is a less hurried course that allows time out for gunk-holing, fishing, viewing old canneries and river towns, or just watching eagles soar. Cruise Ten follows the Washington shore across open waters to Ilwaco. Cruise Eleven follows the Oregon shore along channels past grassy islands.

# Cruise
# Ten

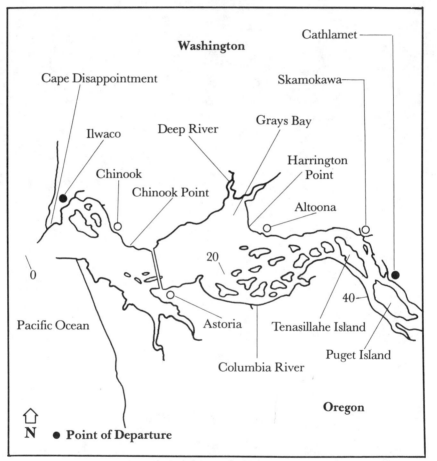

Cathlamet

**Washington**

Cape Disappointment

Skamokawa

Grays Bay

Deep River

Ilwaco

Harrington
Point

Chinook

Chinook Point

Altoona

20

0

40

Pacific Ocean

Astoria

Tenasillahe Island

Puget Island

Columbia River

**Oregon**

N  ● **Point of Departure**

*Do not use for navigation.*
*Use NOAA Nautical Charts 18523 and 18521*

# Cathlamet to Ilwaco

**Point of departure:** Cathlamet, Washington
**Course:** following Washington side of estuary, Columbia main channel via North Channel across Grays Bay to Point Ellice, Chinook Point, Chinook, and Ilwaco
**Stops:** Steamboat Slough, Skamokawa, Deep River, Chinook, Ilwaco
**Length of cruise:** approximately 35 statute miles
**Duration on power:** 1 day
**Duration on sail:** 1 to 2 days
**Overnight moorage:** Steamboat Slough, Skamokawa, Deep River, Chinook, Ilwaco

# Bays and Byways along the Washington Shore

As the Columbia flows around and below Tenasillahe and Welch islands, a few miles west of Cathlamet, it forms a broad estuary filled with islands, sandbars, and shoals. At one point between the Oregon and Washington shores it is eight miles across.

This wide expanse of water prompted Lieutenant Broughton in 1792 to conclude that the mouth of the Columbia was above Tenasillahe Island and not at the bar as claimed by Robert Gray. Gray had sailed the *Columbia Rediviva* across the bar five months earlier and claimed the river for the United States. Broughton thus claimed the river for the British crown. His commanding officer, Vancouver, however, did not agree and credited Gray with the discovery of the river.

Thirteen years later Lewis and Clark standing near the head of the estuary with the wind carrying what could be the sound of waves, exclaimed those now famous words, "O joy the Ocien." But the ocean was still more than twenty miles away.

When you cruise the estuary, keep in mind the tidal influence. The swing here is about six feet. As mentioned before, if you have a taste for gunk-holing or you want to cross a shoaly area, do it as the tide is coming in so that if you should run aground, the incoming tide will lift you off. Because of the six-foot change, the ebbs and floods can also be used to advantage when planning a trip. Move with the tide for an extra push.

The early part of this cruise follows the main channel to Altoona, then leaves the channel and cuts across Grays Bay. From there this cruise takes a side trip into Deep River, then continues along the Washington side under the Astoria Bridge on to Ilwaco.

After you leave the marina, retrace the course on Elochoman Slough that you followed in. Although Elochoman Slough flows north and west around Hunting Islands to the Columbia, it is not navigable the full length. When you exit from the slough, turn west past Hunting Islands to the main channel.

Hunting Islands, Tenasillahe, a portion of Price Island, and some acreage on the Washington mainland comprise the Columbian White-tailed Deer National Wildlife Refuge. It was established in 1972 when the near-extinct deer—distinguished by a long, wide tail with a white undersurface—were discovered in the area. You may go ashore to the refuge and see these deer and other wildlife, including elk. Just tie up in Steamboat Slough near Price Island.

The first recorded sighting of these deer was made by Lewis and Clark. At that time, the deer ranged along the bottomland near rivers and were more abundant than black-tailed deer. In 1980, a survey of thirty-two islands from The Dalles, Oregon, to the refuge showed eighty deer living on five small islands in the lower Columbia. This brought the known number of deer living near the river to about four hundred.

Along the mainland, the low diked rim is part of the refuge, and just down river is the tree-crowded opening to Steamboat Slough. The slough, with its deep, protected waters between the mainland and Price Island, is a favorite moorage for many boaters. As you enter the slough, stay closer to the island side. Deadheads and root stumps lie scattered like gnarled hands on the mainland shore.

The best time to visit the refuge to see the deer is in the early morning or evening. During these hours, the deer graze in the open fields, but at other times they retreat to the protection of the trees. Having secured the boat, you can row the dinghy to the refuge and walk the road that runs along the top of the dike. Our visits have been during midday, but we still were able to see some deer by walking the road west toward the trees. For one instant, they stood staring, their big eyes looking first curiously, then fearfully. Turning, they leaped and flipped their tails up, exposing the white underside as they disappeared into a thicket.

Skamokawa, on the west end of Steamboat Slough, is a history buff's delight. (You can also approach Skamokawa from the main channel below Price Island.) This small community, noted for the number of historic buildings still standing, is one of the few along the Washington shore from here to Ilwaco that survived the demise of the fishing and logging industries, and the change of the "highway" from river to land. Tucked beneath a break between high hills where two sloughs and a river converge at the Columbia River, Skamokawa has been referred to as a miniature Venice. Looking at the small harbor today, it is difficult to imagine that during the town's most prosperous times in the late 1890s, several large schooners lay at anchor waiting to take on cargoes of lumber. The waterway then was the highway. At the west end of Steamboat Slough, a large yellow building, once a store, is evidence of this. Still trim and neat, its hollow front faces down river. When loggers were injured in the woods, they lay on the dock in front of this store to await a boat that would take them to the hospital in Astoria. When the road was built about twenty years later, the business closed and is now located at Hoby's Country Store, which is accessible by both boat and car.

Hoby's dock is next door to a net shet where nets hang drying. The net shed and the back of the store are visible from the river. You can tie up here for an hour or several days; there is no charge, because water and electricity are not available. But nearly every imaginable item a boater needs is available in the store. Boaters who stopped here before 1982, the year Hoby Thacker sold the store, remember the store as "Hoby's." Though the name has changed to Hoby's Country Store, everything else is the same. Hoby has lived in Skamokawa since 1950 and made friends with numerous boaters who tied up at the dock. One family, he said, liked his quiet harbor so well they came each year during berry season, stayed a week, and picked berries for jam making.

Gas is available for small boats at a pump up Brooks Slough beyond a bridge. Skamokawa Vista Park is located a short walk from the store across the highway bridge. You will find tennis courts, picnic tables, jogging track, boat ramp, and solar-heated showers.

Sailing on the Columbia in front of Skamokawa you feel the broad expanse of the river. Massive, timber-cloaked slopes extend along the north shore. To the southwest, the low hummocks of sand and islands appear to run to the end of the horizon.

From here and other places in the estuary, you can look back on a clear day and see snow-topped peaks in the Cascades. The last time we sailed here, we saw Mount Saint Helens, its flanks ash-gray from its preliminary steam and ash venting. The next day, the eighteenth of May, as we returned up river above Cathlamet, we watched the volcano erupt. That day its symmetrical peak was erased from the skyline.

River traffic in the estuary is now quiet compared with historic times. Indians paddled their canoes between villages, square-riggers sailed around the islands, and steamboats carried supplies and passengers to the small river towns. During fishing season in the late 1800s, gill-netters dropped their nets from small sailboats. Carrying butterfly-shaped sails, this fleet of nearly five hundred looked like swarming insects as they scooted across the distant water.

The large headland down river is Jim Crow Point. In a small bay on the east side, Crown Zellerbach had an old log dump. Once the cannery and houses of Brookfield were bunched around the bay, but now they are gone. The water is deep enough here so you can back or nose the boat almost against the cliffs.

As you round Jim Crown Point, you can see a large rock that is twenty-five feet above the water and has a navigational light on top. This is Pillar Rock, located about one thousand feet offshore from a community of the same name. In 1840, the Hudson's Bay Company set up a salmon saltery on shore. The community of Pillar Rock began

*Pillar Rock*

in 1878 solely for the purpose of canning salmon. Since there was little room to build on the steep slopes, saloons, mercantiles, dance halls, and the canneries were built on pilings over the water. Chinese laborers worked in the canneries and lived in a three-story building called "The China House" in Altoona, Pillar Rock's downstream neighbor.

The cannery at Pillar Rock closed in 1947. The rust-red roofs now cover a cavernous interior where gill nets are stored. Although the waters are deep and the scene looks inviting to explore, the cannery is privately owned and well posted with "No Trespassing" signs.

A road built years later connects both communities with a highway, but one family who lived in Pillar Rock in 1980 ran a boat to Astoria for groceries and supplies. In the three miles between Pillar Rock and Altoona, a few newer homes are scattered among the trees, and a well-preserved white Victorian house built in the 1880s can be seen from the river.

Just above Altoona and the old cannery, the main channel swings southwest to Tongue Point and Astoria. Below the cannery, nose the boat toward Harrington Point to cross Grays Bay.

The channel on the chart is called North Channel, and only one buoy is indicated. There are, however, more on the bay. The channel is changeable and shifts about, so the buoys are changed frequently.

Towboaters who use Grays Bay sometimes put out their own channel markers made of twigs and two-by-fours. The depths on the west side of this bay are good.

Beyond Harrington Point, the river sprawls nearly eight miles from Grays Bay on the north to Cathlamet Bay on the south. Low hills fringe the shoreline. In the distance, oddly shaped Saddleback Mountain pushes up against a slate blue sky. Mud flats and marsh grasses, stripped of their water covering at low tide, can be seen in the north end of Grays Bay. Today, these flats cut out almost all boat traffic into Grays River. Nonetheless, boats used to ply this river on a regular schedule into the town of Grays River. They often picked up cans of milk produced by the dairy herds in the neighboring valleys, then delivered them to Astoria.

North Channel ends just above Portuguese Point, a small, picturesque point extending toward the bay on the west side. Tugs work this side pulling log rafts out of Deep River from a log dump upstream. They move into Deep River on an incoming tide, and often wait for a tidal swing to exit back across North Channel.

If you have decided to go into Deep River, you may want to take time to hunt for the town of Frankfort—maybe with the binoculars, since that's the safest way. Located above Portuguese Point, it was visible from the water until wild vegetation began to reclaim the houses and fruit trees. The town was promoted and started in 1890 by two men, both named Frank, who hoped the Northern Pacific Railroad would locate a terminus here. The railroad never came, and the promotion fizzled, but some people stayed on to fish for a living. The last resident was moved to a nursing home in 1962. The only way in and out of Frankfort was by river, and a long dock for many years reached over mud flats to deep water.

Above Rocky Point to the mouth of Deep River, the channel in this northwest corner of the bay is narrow, but marked.

Deep River, its blue-green waters serpenting back into narrow valleys, was named because of its depths of up to fifty feet. Years ago hand loggers used to work around the mouth of the river. About four miles in and beyond the log dump is the community of Deep River. Now slowly becoming a ghost town, it, too, flourished when the river was a highway. There are spots along the river to drop anchor or tie up to a log raft for the night. Because these moist valleys cool quickly as the sun draws its rays from the fields and up the hills, it may be too cool for swimming, but it is a good place to drop a fishing line.

In the morning, the sounds that greet you in this rural setting may be from a barking dog or a crowing rooster. When departing Deep River, two points should be considered: the tide and the wind. Westerly winds pick up later in the morning on the Columbia, so if the tide is right, you might consider leaving early.

Retrace your route to Portuguese Point, then past Grays Point and in front of the small bay toward the point below Knappton. Watch for pilings: some are submerged and marked on the chart. The pilings on the west side of this bay, many visible above the water, are all that remain of Knappton, a sawmill town that stood on this site for eighty years. At one time, homes stood on slopes above the mill and the whine of saws echoed across the bay where sailing ships and steamers hung on mooring lines. In 1941, the mill was destroyed by fire. When the highway was built in 1960, most of the already decaying buildings disappeared.

Below Knappton, you no longer move through or by bays, but follow a course along the edge of open water below hills to the north. Ahead, the Astoria Bridge, its long span looking like a thin line drawn across the water and sky, gradually moves upward as it crosses the river. Its highest point arches over the shipping channel in front of Astoria. The ferry that ended its service when the bridge was completed in the mid-1960s crossed at about the same location.

If you choose to head for Astoria instead of continuing on to Ilwaco, this is the place to cross, next to the bridge. Stay on the west side close to the bridge piers and watch the current and depths.

On the Washington side, the bridge clearance is forty-nine feet. As you continue west down river, watch the chart and stay out from the shore. Chinook Point juts into the river. On a knoll and partly obscured by trees stands Fort Columbia State Park. Military forces concerned with early defense of the mouth of the Columbia built three strategically located forts, the most inland of which was Fort Columbia. The other

*Cape Disappointment Lighthouse at Fort Canby State Park, Washington*

two are Fort Stevens in Oregon and Fort Canby at Cape Disappointment. Construction of the fort began in 1895 and lasted eight years. Gun batteries that were still in place served as coast defense during both world wars, but the guns at Fort Columbia never fired at an enemy.

Before Fort Columbia was built, the point was the home of Chief Concomly and his six wives and many children. Concomly, a Chinook chief, has been called the first Columbia River pilot. When he saw a ship readying to come across the bar, he and his braves launched a canoe and hurried into position to guide the ship across.

The two communities just down river, Chinook and Ilwaco, are both on Baker Bay. Both owe their beginnings and growth to salmon and fishtraps. At one time Baker Bay was filled with fishtraps—the vestiges of some are the submerged pilings marked on the chart, such as those near Knappton. Fishtraps, like fishwheels on the mid-Columbia, were stationary devices used to catch large quantities of salmon. Pilings were driven into the riverbed and nets were hung on the pilings to form a heart, a tunnel, and a pot. A skiff came alongside and lifted the salmon from the pot. The first trap was built in Baker Bay near Ilwaco in 1879. Eventually, many traps stood in the bay and were spotted under water to about Nassa Point above Cathlamet.

When canneries were built to handle the salmon catch from the traps, both Ilwaco and Chinook grew rapidly. At one time there were thirty-nine canneries on the Columbia. In 1883—one of the peak canning years—629,000 cases of salmon were packed. Each case sold for five dollars.

Mel Lebeck, who managed the Chinook Cannery for many years,

*Chinook Packing Company at Chinook, Washington*

told about his father who had a trap near Point Ellice, at the northern edge of the Astoria Bridge. Lebeck recalls that when he was four years old, his father bundled him up in a blanket, put him aboard a skiff, and they set out to retrieve the salmon in the trap. One trap could provide a yearly income for a family. "If you had a good trap [the right location], you could make a good livelihood," he said.

Even though there was an abundance of salmon, gill-netters threatened to go to war against fishtrap owners. In 1896, troops arrived from Olympia and set up camp in Ilwaco. A sixty-three-foot launch armed with a six-inch cannon steamed through the gill net navy, but a shot was never fired. This "war" soon evaporated like the coastal mists, but the bad feelings never waned. Whenever a pile driver drove pilings for a fish trap, a U.S. marshall stood guard.

Fishtraps were voted out in Washington in 1934 and in Oregon a few years later.

Those in the fish industry were concerned about conserving salmon runs, and started hatcheries in the late 1800s. Several were established in Oregon. The oldest one in Washington, abandoned and now used as a fisheries teaching facility, is located up the Chinook River.

Chinook has a small, uncrowded basin shaped by a rock jetty. There is a transient moorage with gas, ice, and supplies available. The majority of boats moored here belong to the fishermen who supply the Chinook Packing Company. Until recently, the company operated as a cannery and was the last of many on the Columbia River. Now it processes fresh and frozen crab, salmon, shrimp, and bottom fish. Before the fishtraps were outlawed, the town of Chinook, with about five hundred residents at the time, was known as the richest per capita town in Washington. Those whose traps were located near the middle of the river got the biggest catches. They were the "leaders of society," and built large, stately homes in Chinook, many of which are still occupied.

Should you decide to take a look at this quiet, century-old town, follow the dredged Chinook Channel shown on the chart. It is marked with buoys and starts about a mile out and southwest of Chinook. The town, its homes standing among trees, is easy to spot. The cannery is an imposing building rising from the low shoreline at the west end of the basin.

Ilwaco, a few miles farther downstream, stands at the lower end of Baker Bay, beneath the forested bluffs that shape Cape Disappointment. The channel into Ilwaco begins near Jetty A and buoy number eleven and runs west of Sand Island. Because the entrance is subject to change, the entrance buoys are not listed on the chart. The channel is about three miles long, and was dredged to sixteen feet in 1985. Watch for currents and a swell as you go in.

At the end of the channel you'll find a port that has plenty of fishing atmosphere. Clustered in the large mooring basin are fishing boats of all descriptions, charter boats, and some pleasure boats. Fish processing and packing plants stand near the west end of the basin. At Jesse's Ilwaco Fish Company, a large salmon-pink building, a viewing window has been cut in the side of the building. Visitors can watch the skillful hands of women as they filet sole in three quick cuts, shake crab, or prepare whatever fish the boats have brought in that day.

There is transient moorage in the basin, which is operated by the Port of Ilwaco. Gas and diesel are available, and it is a short two-block walk into town for groceries or other needs. When you pull in and tie up, inquire at the port office for overnight space. Their office hours between Memorial Day and Labor Day are from 8:00 A.M. to 5:00 P.M. seven days a week. You might even ask for two nights, since there is much to see and enjoy in Ilwaco and the northern part of Long Beach Peninsula.

A daily bus service runs from the port up the peninsula to the communities of Seaview, Long Beach, and historic Oysterville. The bus also connects with Greyhound in Astoria. Ask at the port for schedules.

In Seaview, the Shelburne Inn is a place worth stopping at for lunch, dinner, or overnight. Built in 1896, it is one of the few surviving Victorian hotels in southwest Washington. From the menu you can sample local seafood including salmon, clams, and oysters, wild mushrooms and berries, homemade jams and jellies, and fresh baked bread. Overnight guests stay in rooms furnished with antiques. Call (206) 642-2442 for overnight reservations. Call (206) 642-4142 for lunch or dinner reservations.

At Long Beach, a beach resort town for nearly a century, stop at the Milton York Candy Company and try their hand-dipped chocolates made with a thick cream and butter. The company, in operation since the late 1800s, also offers tours through their candy-making rooms. From their delicatessen, they serve a creamy clam chowder and other fare for lunch and dinner.

The bus line ends at Oysterville. This village, established in 1854, faces Willapa Bay. The first residents harvested the rich oyster beds and sent the bounty to San Francisco. Some houses outlined with picket fences date back to 1860.

In Ilwaco you can stroll the quiet residential streets past homes built by fishermen in the late 1880s, or stop at the Ilwaco Heritage Museum to learn about the town's beginnings. A longer walk—about three miles—takes you to the last Lewis and Clark Interpretive Center on the inland waterway. The road to Fort Canby State Park and the center skirts the lower end of Baker Bay and rises up the hillside into the woods. The center overlooks the Pacific Ocean and is located on the site of the old coastal defense batteries. It also has displays telling the story of the first Coast Guard lifesaving station, when men put out in rowboats to save those on ships wrecked on or near the bar. The Coast Guard station, charged with the same duty today, is located on the southwest arm of Baker Bay.

Here, as in Warrenton or Hammond, Oregon, you can get on a charter boat to go across the bar to fish for salmon or tuna. Unless you are familiar with the bar and its navigation, it is safer to go on a charter than to try crossing the bar on your own.

Good fishing is also available inside the bar. Fishermen launch their boats at Ilwaco to fish for salmon, particularly in late summer, when they are found in large numbers near the mouth of the Columbia.

If you want to take a shorter route to return up river when you leave Ilwaco, follow the main shipping channel after you clear buoy number eleven.

## Cruise
# Eleven

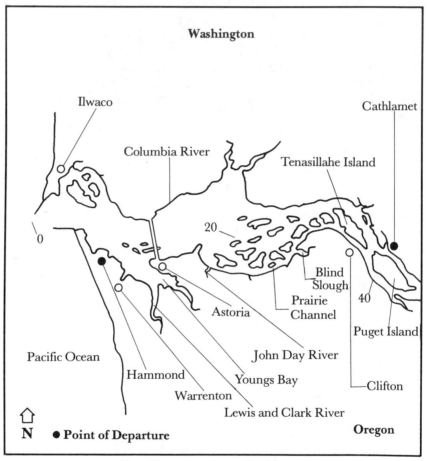

Do not use for navigation.
Use NOAA Nautical Charts 18523 and 18521

# Cathlamet to Hammond

**Point of departure:** Cathlamet, Washington

**Course:** Following Oregon side of the estuary, Clifton Channel to Prairie Channel, through Cathlamet Bay to Tongue Point, then via the main channel to Astoria, Warrenton, and Hammond

**Stops:** Blind Slough, Astoria, Warrenton, Hammond

**Length of cruise:** approximately 30 statute miles

**Duration on power:** 1 day

**Duration on sail:** 1 day

**Overnight moorage:** Astoria, Warrenton, Hammond

# Islands and Channels along the Oregon Shore

To sample the Oregon side of the estuary, this trip follows channels, with a side trip up Blind Slough, and then cruises the open waters beyond Tongue Point to Astoria and Hammond. The distance without side trips is about thirty miles.

In these estuary waters and for a short way up river, you may encounter, during early spring, the shiny head of a harbor seal. These mammals come into the river in the winter and leave after the run of spring Chinook. Although they may appear to be charming, whiskered, water sprites, to the local fishermen they are the scourge of the water. Blamed for fish-kill and damaged nets, they carry little charm for local fishermen.

To enter Clifton Channel, which flows beneath foothills, cut south around the lower end of Puget Island across the main channel. The entrance is easy to spot as it lies north of pilings that supported a bygone mill or fish receiving station. This same passage from Cathlamet to the Oregon bank was the early settlers' link with the outside world. Cathlamet and Puget Island folks were not tied by roads to the rest of Washington, and boats came to Clifton for mail. Social activities also drew settlers across to Clifton and, later, to Bradwood. Both are now only ghost towns.

Bradwood, located in the south corner where Clifton Channel takes off from the river, was started in 1930 by the Bradley-Woodward Lumber Company, which was charged with developing a mill and a community. Today, as you cruise by, you can see the tips of the incongruous line of electric light poles. They march in isolation along the main street of the town, now home for five families.

The sand beaches along here are a favorite sunbathing and swimming area, as well as a good fishing spot for steelhead and salmon. You can anchor out, but watch for the wake of passing freighters from the main channel.

Downstream from Bradwood are the remnants of the much older community of Clifton. One of the first salmon canneries was built here in 1874. Cliffs behind the town may have been the reason for its name.

Along this brief stretch between Bradwood and Clifton, where eagles soar and rest in treetops, it is quiet, almost deserted now compared with earlier times. Five small logging camps and mills were located here, as were fish stations and sheds for horses used in seining. There were pockets of ethnic groupings: Greektown was upstream on the channel, then Slovak town, and Italian town. The alien law of 1921 forced most out, since they could not fish unless they were citizens.

A few family names are still reminders of these early settlers. The Marincoviches lived on the edge of the channel near a boat dock and net sheds. Andrew lived here on the river all his seventy-plus years. He began to fish when he was fourteen, and sold his gill net boat when he was sixty-nine. He remembered the old days on the river, and with a knowing smile recounted times of lusty excitement and of bone-wearing depression. His fingers moved in silent drumming on the table when he recalled the cold winter nights he spent huddled on the docks stripping the smelt one by one from the tiny mesh of the nets—and not getting enough cash to pay for his time.

Tenasillahe Island is to starboard. The name is Chinook jargon for "small land." When it was first settled, it was a small, idyllic community. The island was diked in 1907, and the marshes turned to meadows where dairy cattle grazed. About twenty people lived here then, and there was a small cheese factory. An old picture album shows neatly cropped lawns and immaculate barns. Later a holding company bought the island to raise beef cattle, then it was sold to the government to be turned into a wildlife refuge. The dikes broke, but have since been repaired to improve the habitat for the Columbian white-tailed deer.

*Net shed near the Columbia River estuary*

A good place to try gunk-holing is Multnomah Slough between Welch and Tenasillahe islands. But watch the depth sounder and the tides. We have known skippers who had to back their sailboats out of the slough.

Clifton Channel makes a wide swing around Aldrich Point. Follow the chart and do not cut too close to the point. South, near the downstream end of Tronson Island, begin to angle across to Horseshoe Island. Along this shore at Devils Elbow, the stream has scoured out good depths almost to the banks of the island. There are good depths for cruising through Clifton and Prairie channels, but you have to be careful. When we cruise these channels, one crew member reads the chart while the skipper, hand on the tiller, watches the depth sounder and the water ahead.

If you're willing to take a short detour below Tronson Island, you'll have a chance to see some living history. In the waterway northwest of Tronson and between Woody and Horseshoe islands there are a few families still living in float houses. The gray, oblong houses, always sagging a bit on one side, have a small dinghy turned upside down on the porch, nets and floats stored to the side, and perhaps a curl of smoke rising from the chimney.

Near some houses here and elsewhere in the area, you may see bluestone tubs. Like the sturdy hand-patched nets of earlier times, bluestone tubs are a remnant of fishing's better days. These weathered wooden tubs were used for soaking nets in a sodium chloride solution to

*Float houses on the John Day River*

help preserve the net fibers.

Few people live here anymore. Life here can be harsh as winds whip up the river, and in winter thick fog enfolds the islands. Fishing has dropped off, the industry almost gone, but a few hardy individuals still cling to an independent lifestyle. There are a few other float houses around the islands, occupied during a few summer months or visited once or twice a year.

Resist the temptations to pick up charming souvenirs such as net needles or floats lying on what appear to be deserted net sheds. No matter how dilapidated the structures look, someone owns them. This is a small, tight, secluded culture on the lower estuary. It is a fascinating culture embroidered with customs, beliefs, and working patterns born of years spent on the river fishing and in the mountains logging.

After exploring the area of Woody Island, retrace your route back to the channel. Near the end of Devils Elbow, a grasslined bank on Horseshoe Island, head across Prairie Channel to a boathouse on the mainland (shown as Long Island on the chart) before continuing a course along Prairie Channel. This angling across the channel avoids shallows off Horseshoe.

Continue below Marsh Island into Knappa Slough, a quiet tree-lined backwater. Then to get into Blind Slough, go below the islands at the mouth and come back along the south shore.

One historian feels that this slough was so named because it wanders for several miles and arrives nowhere in particular. One larger branch just suddenly ends. The slough is a slow, wide swath through verdant dairy country, dotted with the river's counterpart of "wide spots in the road" moorage communities. Although still a back road of boating, its tempo picks up slightly as fishermen bring in their boats.

Small boats can explore the narrow water pathways that join Blind Slough. Many end by petering out in some farm's backyard. For deeper draft boats, cruising is good along the main branch beyond the railroad swing bridge left open except when a train passes by. The bridge is an example of the comfortable, no-rush atmosphere here: electricity reached the bridge operator in 1979.

Out of Blind Slough, with the bow pointed down Knappa Slough, you make a wide swing in front of Knappa where a house stands on a short bluff near an old dock. Beyond Knappa, there are two ways around Minaker Island, both of which will bring you back onto Prairie Channel. The deeper water is on the north side.

As you've noticed, people are drawn to these protected waterways to live on or next to them. Here, where houses are less exposed to the wind in a setting softened by trees and wild shrubs, they are, in most cases, a contrast to the austere float houses on Woody Island. A few such houses are located in the channel behind Svensen Island, on the

*Knappa Slough*

southern loop of Prairie Channel, and more houses are along John Day River.

The best way to see the island or the river is in a small powerboat. Entering Svensen Island Channel is a bit tricky because of silting, but as you edge the boat into the passage, you find yourself in a traditional lower Columbia inlet, with a tiny enclave of fishing boats and boathouses. Colors and even sounds here are muted. Small, one-man fishing boats pick their way back up the channel headed toward splintered docks and houseboats where nets hang draped and drying on wide porches.

The safest approach to John Day River is to proceed northwest across the upper side of Cathlamet Bay to Tongue Point, then cut back in front of Mott Basin, an old military dock area used during World War II.

Across the mouth of the John Day River is a Burlington Northern swing bridge that is also operated by hand. Like the Clatskanie River and Blind Slough bridges, this bridge is also left open unless a train clatters by.

A thriving strip city of houseboats lines the river in a cheerful parade. Small and rustic, they also reflect the time and people of this area. Swatches of color abound—a red geranium in a rusty coffee can, a brilliant blue door—shouting out in defiance of what can be four winter months of constant gray rain and fog.

When you proceed from the lower end of Cathlamet Bay toward Tongue Point—a high, rocky peninsula covered with trees—watch for stumps, snags, and shoals and keep track of the tide, which in this delta country alternately exposes and covers many of them. Under noonday sun, the exposed shoals blend with the wrinkled-water patterns. From a distance, you hardly realize the shoals are there until a gull drops from the wind and stands on one.

Turning the corner around Tongue Point, you'll see Astoria ahead. The scene may be a surprise after the quiet cruise along the byways. If it is a windy day, the winds, no longer diminished by islands and trees, blow stronger across the open water. The boat is buffeted by winds and tossed by heavier chop. Large freighters may be moving in or out of berths, or swing on an anchor in the harbor. Astoria rises on a hill above the harbor and spreads across the peninsula between the river and Youngs Bay. On the top of its 700-foot hill stands a 125-foot spire, the Astor Column. To commemorate Astoria's colorful past, historic events are illuminated on a frieze that circles the main portion of this spire.

Astoria's history began in 1811. Men working for John Jacob Astor's Pacific Fur Company built a post here then and named it Astoria. It was the first American commercial settlement on the Pacific Coast. The British renamed the post Fort George when they took it over in 1813, but five years later it was returned to the Americans, and the original name was eventually restored.

Looking at the graceful Victorian architecture of the restored homes, it is difficult to understand why passengers on sternwheelers considered Astoria only a place where they could change boats, then continue on to someplace else. The town, with its waterfront made up of docks and stilts over mud flats and its sawmilling and fishing, apparently had no appeal to summer tourists headed for ocean beaches.

Today, Astoria offers excellent moorage and interesting onshore activities. The East Basin, about two miles above the bridge, has fifty berths but no services. If you are going to take on any supplies, however, a stop there affords easy access to a large supermarket.

West Basin, about one-third mile below the bridge, is the largest and one of the best equipped public moorages on the river. Besides all the usual amenities, it has an excellent dockside restaurant and access to picturesque and historic Astoria. You might want to spend a night on shore or just an evening out. Both are possible at the Thunderbird Motel overlooking the basin.

To test once again the feel of land, take a walking tour of Astoria. The tour is described in a pamphlet available at the Chamber of Commerce. Also, a visit to the Historical Museum and the Maritime Museum is a choice way to spend some interesting hours. For directions, check with one of the local residents.

One unique feature of the Maritime Museum is the old lightship *Columbia,* which stood as a sentinel off the bar for many years. As you tour the ship and stand in the cramped quarters, you can imagine spending months of duty there, pitching up and down in waters known for their turbulence. The museum also includes extensive displays of ship models and nautical gear of all sorts. For anyone who loves boats or boating, it is a gold mine of artifacts.

For a final tour de force, plan on eating at the Fiddlers Green, located right under the bridge pillars on the waterfront. Its setting is part of the history of the area—ask any of the employees of this delightful establishment to describe the early days of shanghaiing.

Although it may seem this is the last port before crossing the bar, there are two more west of Astoria—Warrenton and Hammond. Both have basins where transients can moor, and both serve as home for large charter fleets.

As you proceed west in the main shipping channel, you'll come to a wide shallow bay to the south. This is Youngs Bay, the outlet for Youngs River and the Lewis and Clark River. Lieutenant Broughton explored Youngs River and named it for Sir George Young of the Royal Navy. Lewis and Clark called the bay Meriwether Bay for Lewis, but that name was never commonly used. The name of the Lewis and Clark River did become generally accepted, however, after these two and their men departed on their return trek in 1806. Lewis and Clark built Fort Clatsop on the river two miles upstream from its mouth. They spent the winter of 1805–1806 here, and left at 1:00 P.M. Sunday, 23 March 1806.

If you choose to explore Youngs Bay, follow the marked channel. There are two bridges in the north end, a highway bridge (clearance forty-five feet), and a railroad bridge (clearance seventeen feet).

The entrance to Warrenton is just west of Youngs Bay. At the lower end of an improved channel on the Skipanon Waterway, you'll find marinas with all services available, including showers at the Skipanon Marina. A restaurant and quick-serve market are nearby.

Warrenton, whose beginnings reach back to 1848, is proud that in 1912 the townspeople elected the first woman mayor west of the Rockies. Also, the first woman city manager in the nation served here in 1923.

At Hammond, a little over two miles west of the entrance to Warrenton, there is a circular basin with two hundred berths and a launch ramp. Supplies, including gas and diesel, are also available.

If you are an avid fisherman, you may want to cross the bar to do some ocean fishing. Unless you are familiar with these waters, however, it is safer to cross the bar in a charter boat than to go in your own. The bar is infamous worldwide for its treachery and difficult navigation. If you do not take a charter out of Hammond or Warrenton, you can take one from Ilwaco, Washington, where the larger charter fleet is berthed. To reach Ilwaco from Hammond, continue in the shipping channel to Jetty A near buoy number eleven. Then proceed as described in Cruise Ten.

This point may mark the end of your descent of the Columbia-Snake Inland Waterway. To the west, the waters of the Snake, the Palouse, the Deschutes, and the Columbia merge with the waters of the Pacific. Now you, like the early explorers, have traveled the "River of the West."

# The Shaping of the Rivers: A Geologic Overview

The Columbia River, apparently so entrenched in its course, has been shaped by both slow and cataclysmic changes over millions of years. To the north in British Columbia, it flows through a complex series of ranges and high plateaus known as the Columbia-Rocky Mountains. Entering Washington, it cuts through a region known as the Columbia Plateau. To the west it breaches the Cascades and merges with the Willamette River in the Puget-Willamette Lowlands before it finally breaks through the Coast Range to the sea.

The precise age of the river has not been determined, but water-rounded pebbles of rock like those found in eastern Oregon and British Columbia are embedded in formations found near Astoria. These deposits suggest an ancestral Columbia River flowing to the sea in early Pliocene time, nearly 5 million years ago. Since that time, the Columbia and its ancestors have worn their way to the sea, persevering against the slow building of mountains and events of catastrophic scale.

The oldest rocks along the Columbia River are found in the Columbia-Rocky Mountains of extreme northern Washington and southeastern British Columbia. From the Pre-Cambrian era, over 800 million years ago, to the end of the Mesozoic era, about 65 million years ago, this region marked the western edge of the North American continent. The environment was subtropical, much like that of today's Gulf Coast. Early in this long period, well-stratified beds of limestone, sandstone, and quartz sandstone were gradually laid down. They are up to fifty thousand feet thick in some places. Toward the end of the Mesozoic era, massive folding and faulting occurred. Over millions of years, faults hundreds of miles long were active, and entire mountain ranges were folded. The original rocks were changed by heat and pressure, and molten rock welled up to cool and crystallize beneath the surface.

The geologic history of the primordial sea west of the Columbia-Rocky Mountain Region is not clear, since the rock record is buried deep beneath the strata laid down over the last 65 million years. Some data support the existence of an offshore archipelago in the present area of the Cascades and Coast Range while the Columbia-Rocky Mountains were slowing building at the continent's edge. Other data suggest that what is now the western edge of the continent was once oceanic crust that vaulted and rose against the continental plate.

In any case, by the beginning of the Cenozoic era, 65 million years ago, the shallow seas had retreated from eastern Oregon and Washington. The rocks forming the Columbia-Rocky Mountains were in place and the stage was set for the creation of the landforms we see today.

At the beginning of this period, submarine volcanoes were where the Coast Range now is. The Puget-Willamette Lowlands were a broad coastal plain where figs, palms, and avocados grew, eventually creating the commercial coal and gas deposits found in the area today. Over millions of years, a line of active volcanoes along the present Cascades spread thousands of feet of volcanic rubble both east and west of the crest.

The last major volcanic activity in the Coast Range began during the Eocene epoch, some 50 million years ago. Over the next 15 million years, major underwater eruptions produced the marine basalts known as the Crescent Formation. Later altered by folding and compression, the flows are the thickest volcanic flows known, equaling the volume of five thousand Mount Rainiers. While not visible along the Columbia, they are the predominant rock of the Olympic Mountains to the north.

Coast Range volcanism ceased, but the line of volcanoes along the Cascades persisted. The shallow western sea retreated farther and the climate, though still subtropical, became more temperate. Cascade crest volcanism alternated with deep weathering. The deep red bed seen above Stevenson, Washington, was deposited during this period about 30 million years ago. Volcanic eruptions of mud and ash were occurring on the Columbia Plateau, and the Columbia-Rocky Mountains continued to be affected by folding, faulting, and some volcanic overlays.

Then, about 17 million years ago, in the middle Miocene period, a series of north-south fissures opened along the eastern edge of the Columbia Plateau. For the next 7 million years, these fissures produced the largest outpouring of lava ever to occur in North America. These lavas, known as the Columbia River Basalt Group, form the dark, forbidding cliffs along the Columbia and Snake rivers from the Okanogan Valley to near the mouth of the Columbia. The two Cape Horns on the lower Columbia are composed of this same basalt.

Typical flows were one hundred to two hundred feet thick. The molten lava moved about twenty-five to thirty miles an hour, burning everything in its path. Cooling of each flow took several decades, and the process produced forms that are visible today. The lower portion of a separate flow is characteristically composed of vertical columns two feet or more in diameter. The upper portion is composed of regular but smaller columns that are often inclined or fan-shaped. The topmost section is porous, and resulted from escaping gas. Agates and thunder eggs are formed by gradual groundwater precipitation of minerals in the vesicles, or cavities, in the volcanic rock.

The warm, moist climate soon transformed the tops of each flow into a more hospitable environment. Soil formed, vegetation returned, and animals regained the land—all to be buried by the next flow. A perfect cast of a burned rhinoceros has been found at the bottom of a basalt flow near Grand Coulee.

Despite these flows and concurrent downwarping and folding, the ancestral Columbia continued working its way to the sea. In the Big Bend west of Grand Coulee, the river cut through the folding as it occurred. In other areas, the folds diverted the river. The Rattlesnake Hills, for example, diverted it east toward Wallula.

The last outpouring of Columbia River basalt was followed by a long period of relative quiet. Some volcanoes continued in the Columbia Plateau, but deep weathering and erosion occurred along the Cascades. A thick floodwater deposit of coarse sand and gravels was built over the subsiding Puget-Willamette Lowlands and in basins to the east. Known as the Troutdale Formation, it is composed of local rocks and polished quartzite pebbles from the metamorphosed Pre-Cambrian rocks of the Columbia-Rocky Mountains. This formation is visible in many areas within the gorge. At Cape Horn, west of Beacon Rock, it can be seen between Columbia River basalt and more recent lavas.

Beginning in the late Pliocene, about 3 million years ago, the region drained by the river had over 300 million years of geologic history behind it, but several major events of different types were yet to come that would produce the river environment we see today.

First, volcanism returned to the Cascades, and Mount Hood and Mount Adams began to build. Early in this period, hundreds of small volcanoes, both east and west of the Cascades, poured out gray, basaltic lavas. These produced Larch Mountain and Mount Defiance east of the Sandy River. Beacon Rock is the southern flank of a basaltic dike built during this period.

As the Cascade volcanoes continued to erupt, sometimes damming the river, the region to the west of the central Columbia Plateau was affected by major uplifting, folding, and faulting. The Coast Range and Cascades were arched upward. In the gorge area, the Troutdale Formation was elevated 2,700 feet, and the originally level Columbia basalts were distorted. Lava columns formed in cooling were tilted, and the tops of the flows were inclined over long distances.

At mile 180, across the river from Mayer State Park, the extreme results of this activity can be seen. At this point a fault breaks a gentle uplift forming a series of vertical hogbacks. At least four separate Columbia River basalt flows have been rotated nearly 180 degrees, and the rock squeezed and broken.

As these processes continued, the world climate began to cool. The rising Cascades intercepted moisture-laden storms from the west. The Columbia Plateau became drier, and today's plant forms began to emerge.

About 2 million years ago, at the beginning of the Pleistocene epoch, the earth's cooling accelerated. Great sheets of ice developed, at times covering up to one-third of the globe. Moisture that had previously returned to the sea as runoff became trapped in ice. Sea level dropped by three hundred feet, steepening the river's gradient and causing deep channels to be cut.

There were four major ice advances, with intervening retreats. The last advance, and the most extensive, occurred forty thousand years ago. It came as far south as the Columbia Plateau, with one ice lobe extending nearly to Wenatchee. In each of the four periods, the Columbia-Rocky Mountains were inundated by ice up to eight thousand feet thick. The environment was like that of Antarctica today. This glacial scouring produced the broad U-shaped valleys of the Rocky Mountain trench, the Selkirks, and the Monashees.

In the higher Cascade peaks, glaciers developed, and many still remain. Glaciers from Mount Hood extended down the Sandy River and also into the Hood River Valley. Larch Mountain and Mount Defiance were sculptured by glaciers. Prior to its 1980 eruption, Mount Saint Helens retained its symmetry as a result of being more recent and thus unaffected by major glacial scarring.

Major flooding occurred along the full length of the lower Columbia in the spring and early summers during the millions of years of each glacial advance, gradually deepening the river and its tributaries. During the interglacial periods, which were warm and arid, the fine, glacial-scoured silt was redistributed by winds to form the thick Palouse soils of eastern Washington.

Near the end of the last ice age, approximately twelve thousand years ago, the last and perhaps most catastrophic events reshaped the lower Columbia. At least twice, and perhaps up to forty times, the northern ice sheet extended far enough south to block the Clark Fork River east of Lake Pend Oreille. These ice dams reached heights of a thousand feet, and produced lakes that extended deep into Montana and were nearly half the size of Lake Michigan. Periodically the ice dams broke, releasing hundreds of cubic miles of water.

The last of these floods, known as the Spokane Floods, swept the ice dam away in a few hours. The water surged to the southwest across the Columbia Plateau; its volume was equivalent to ten times the present flow of all the world's rivers. The water spread up the plateau, forming large lakes in the Yakima and Walla Walla basins, then rolled southeastward up the Snake River Valley. Fanning westward, the waters covered the Umatilla basin, then cut for the gorge. At constrictions within the gorge, hydrostatic damming occurred as the water piled upon itself in its rush to the sea. After breaching the gorge, the water flowed both west and south, forming a large lake as far south as Eugene, Oregon.

The existence of these floods was first proposed by a geologist named Bretz. The theory was disputed for years, but with continued study the evidence for such floods accumulated. This evidence is visible to boaters.

The hanging waterfalls in the gorge are the result of rapid widening that cut away the lower courses of tributary streams. The bare, terraced basalts east of the gorge were produced as the floods stripped away the overlying rocks and soil. Northwest of The Dalles, look for a distinct vegetation line about one thousand feet above the river. Below the line, little vegetation can grow where the soil has been washed away by the flood. The channeled "scablands," including many dry waterfalls, between the Snake and Columbia rivers were scoured by the floods.

The large, erratic boulder that lies in Roosevelt Park is one of thousands of large rocks rafted from Montana in blocks of ice and deposited as the floods receded.

With the end of the ice age and the last of the Spokane Floods, the water held as ice was released to the sea. The lower river gradient became less steep, and tidal influence returned up river to near Portland, leaving a deep drowned channel to be filled by later sedimentation.

Geologic forces continue to shape the Columbia River. Only seven hundred years ago, as determined by tree stump dating, a series of large landslides occurred within the Columbia Gorge. Perhaps with earthquakes as triggers, some of the oldest rocks in the gorge gave way.

The largest slide flowed across the river just east of Bonneville and accounts for the sharp southern turn in the river across from Cascade Locks. This geologic origin was properly deduced by Lewis and Clark on their descent of the river in 1805. The rapids, which the explorers found so difficult to portage, also gave rise to the name of this mountain range—the Cascades—which the river breaches.

And now, Mount Saint Helens has been changed forever by a series of violent eruptions. The magnitude of these recent events gives the boater a better appreciation of the massive scale of the forces of fire, water, and ice that have shaped the Columbia and Snake rivers.

# Cruising and Safety
## on the Inland Waterway

Compared with other western boating waters, the Columbia-Snake Inland Waterway is unique. It is the longest navigable route to the interior. Cutting across diverse geographic and climatic areas as it does, it offers a blend of boating variables that can be challenging, sometimes dangerous, and usually enjoyable. The variables include tides, currents, winds, commercial traffic, and locking-through the dams. Boaters need to be aware of these variables and know how to anticipate and handle them to ensure safe, comfortable, pleasurable cruising.

The waterway's currents are affected by several factors. The downhill run of the river imparts a natural flow that can be impeded by the dams. The current is increased by freshets or the release of water through the turbines or over the spillways. During summer months, there is little current on the Snake, but near the dams at times of freshets or release, the currents will sometimes reach six to eight knots.

These water releases are controlled by the Bonneville Power Administration from a central control point in Vancouver, Washington. The U.S. Army Corps of Engineers has set maximum and minimum water levels behind each dam. Turbine stocks are opened to produce electricity and, occasionally, water is spilled to balance the total system. Releases have a side effect for boaters: behind dams, water levels may vary four to five feet over a few hours' time. This unpredictability needs to be considered when anchoring or gauging vertical clearances under the bridges in the lakes behind dams.

Tidal action occurs from the mouth of the Columbia to the foot of Bonneville Dam, a distance of 145 miles. The farther you are upstream, the lesser the tide's effect. The mean range of tide at Astoria is near six feet; at Longview, three feet; and above Portland, one foot.

Tidal currents will interact with the river's current, and at times you will find the Columbia's flow going up river on a strong incoming tide. On the other hand, an outgoing tide will increase the current. Knowing when these incoming and outgoing tides occur can be used to advantage when you are planning a cruise. If you are down river and returning up river, ride with the incoming tide. It neutralizes the effects of the river's current and will increase your speed returning up river.

Not realizing the effects of tide and current on our second day on the Columbia, we broke out the sails and began tacking up river in light airs. Looking at a mark along the shore, we soon discovered we were going backward.

Tidal currents should also be considered when trying unknown waters. Explore on an incoming tide, particularly in the estuary. If you go aground, better to be waiting for more water than watching what little you have slowly move out to sea. Also, check the tide tables before anchoring in a slough or near a shallow shoreline.

The combination of a strong outgoing tide and spring runoff may cause problems for small boats. During these conditions, stay clear of the pile dikes found on the lower Columbia. These dikes, built by the Corps of Engineers, extend toward the main channel. They direct the current to the river's center, helping to scour the channel and reduce bank erosion. A small boat with little power can get pinned against the piling and have difficulty in getting free.

Current-watching can give you good navigational hints. Outside dredged areas, the channel will be deepest where the current's flow is strongest. An example of this occurs at Devils Elbow in Prairie Channel in the estuary. The scouring effect along the river's outside curve allows even a deep draft boat to move almost up to the shoreline.

Winds are another companion of the waterway boater. Summertime winds generally blow from the west, winter winds from the southeast and east. From any direction, winds tend to follow the river's channel and seldom provide long reaches for the sailboater. Westerly or easterly winds occasionally become strong in the Columbia Gorge where the land formation acts like a giant flue. Here and elsewhere on the Columbia, winds blowing against the current kick up large waves that can cause problems for boaters. Should winds begin to blow while you are cruising, you can duck into the coves and havens that have been mentioned in each cruise section of the book.

The Columbia is one of the greatest dirt movers in the country. Because the Columbia and Snake are a navigable waterway, their main shipping channels are continually maintained by dredging. Some of the islands in both rivers are sand or gravel left by the dredging.

Outside the dredged channel, shoals continue to build and shift. Any place where the current has slowed, the sediment has increased. The low ends of islands should be given a wide berth, as well as the jetties.

Should you go aground, it will most likely be in soft mud or sand. The first action should be: powerboats shift to neutral, sailboats drop or luff the sails. After a quick check to see if you are taking on water, start refloating action. Rocking the boat with crew weight is usually the next step. Sometimes, if the forward motion of the boat is caught in time, the gentle rocking will break the hold of the soft bottom and release you.

Throwing out an anchor and pulling yourself off (called kedging) is another possibility. If you can't throw the anchor out far enough, row it out, or float it out on a life jacket. On sailboats, crew members can hang on a boom swung outward. Or sometimes the water around the shoal is shallow, and you can climb out and push or tug the boat loose. Finally, if you are aground in tidewater, check the tide tables. If the tide is coming in, just wait to be lifted off. Once you are on your way again, mark that spot on the chart.

Charts and the river's many navigational aids are a great help when traveling the waterway. In addition to red and black buoys (leave the red buoys to the left when proceeding down river) there are frequent "day markers" on both shores. Easily noted from the water, these triangular markers are green with odd numbers on the north shore and orange with even numbers on the south, or "right returning," shore. There are also lighted orange panels with black center stripes. Called "range markers," they are set in pairs, one behind the other. When the stripes or lights are lined up, the boater knows he is in mid-channel. All the aids are noted on the charts, so a boater using the charts can always determine his location. Use up-to-date charts and watch for revisions since aids are sometimes added or relocated.

Sometimes these aids to navigation may look like a good place to tie up but it is illegal to do so.

While the waterway channels are well marked and well maintained, they are also well used. Pleasure boats share the waterway with a variety of commercial craft, from ocean-going freighters to small tugs. Commercial traffic has the right of way, including right of way over boats under sail. It is your responsibility to look out for these large vessels. Is is obviously common sense to give freighters and tugs a wide berth at all times. When you are traveling the main channel, you have room to maneuver; large vessels do not. Most of the freighter traffic moves at about ten to fourteen knots. At a speed of ten knots, a ship travels about the length of three football fields in one minute.

The channels are deep enough for commercial traffic, but the width is just enough for easy handling, and does not allow for evasive action. Any such action by a large vessel may put it aground, as may a forced reduction of its speed. The ship needs the action of the propeller wash on the rudder for control. Even if the engines are put into reverse, their forward movement continues for some distance and time.

Captains on the bridge cannot see all that moves directly in front of them. A small boat close to the hull cannot be seen at all. Pleasure boaters who dart in and out are playing with a lumbering giant. If a skier falls one thousand feet in front of a ship going ten knots, he has only one minute to get out of the way. Sailboats who sail too close will have their wind "stolen" and lose manuevering ability. The warning signal given by commercial ships and tugs if a pleasure boat is in the way is four short blasts.

For those who have beached their boats or moored to log rafts near the shipping channel, the wake of passing ships may cause some problem. A strong suction follows the wake as water is pulled from shore to fill the "hole" left by the displacement of the ship. Beach towels and picnic baskets piled on the shore too close to the water may be drawn back into the current.

If you want information about commercial traffic, keep your VHF radio tuned to channel sixteen or thirteen. Someone may be trying to tell you to move over.

Much of the lower waterway traffic, and all of it on the upper reaches, is moved by tugs. Most tugs on the waterway push their "tow," but a tug without a barge in front could be towing log rafts that are hard to see. The careless boater may look directly behind the tug, see nothing, take off, and run into a towline.

Night travelers should know that tugs display different combinations of lights depending on the length of the vessel and the length of its tow. If you want to determine whether you are in the path of a ship or tow, note the sidelights rather than the masthead lights. If you see only one sidelight, or if one is brighter than the other, you can be fairly sure you are not in the direct path. This also gives you an indication of which way to move in order to stay clear. Also, tugs pushing barges are now required to install a flashing amber light in the center of the tow on the lead barge. Some commercial vessels may neglect to show running lights. If you hear the guttural engine throb, watch and stay clear.

A navigable waterway coupled with the adjoining land transportation routes introduces the need for drawbridges. The law requires that all bridges on navigable waters be opened on request by either pleasure or commercial craft. The usual procedure when approaching a drawbridge is to blow one long blast followed by a short one. The tender will acknowledge with one long blast. If you hear four short blasts, it means the bridge cannot open immediately. Signs are posted near the railroad bridges over less used waters indicating how to get in touch with the tender if no one is there. Main channel bridges are tended all the time.

Through the long descent of the waterway there are eight dams to lock-through, four on the Snake and four on the Columbia. The locking procedure is the same for all: if commercial traffic is waiting to lock-through, it has first priority. If one tug is not carrying hazardous material, however, and there is room to lock, pleasure boaters can lock with it.

Presently, even a single pleasure boat can lock-through at any time with no more than an hour's wait, but this may change, since the Corps of Engineers is considering limited hours for pleasure boats. Each lockage uses approximately forty-three million gallons of water— sufficient volume, when run through the dam's turbine, to generate enough power for the average household for six months. There is also a possibility of lengthy delays during a water shortage. Some dams then will have only two or three lockages a day just for pleasure boaters.

Before starting on a cruise that requires passage across a dam, check with the Corps of Engineers to find out if they have started locking restrictions for pleasure boats. Also, the locks are closed for scheduled repairs at times during the year, usually in early spring.

You can contact the lock tender on radio over VHF channel fourteen for instructions. Or, if you have no radio, pull the cord on the small craft signal station just outside the lock. An operator will answer on an intercom. Red and green signal lights are used for visual direction.

Reduce speed when entering the locking area. Tie your boat to the floating mooring bitts, being sure to tie to the floating ones and not to the stationary ladders. Pull on the bitts to see if they move. To ease damage to your chines, place bumpers alongside. Keep checking the lines to see that there are no hang-ups. If you raft together while going through, be sure the lines have slack so boats will not bind. Usual lockage time is about thirty minutes. A short whistle blast is the signal to cast off from the moorings and move out of the locks. Do not dally around either above or below dams. Some boaters are unaware of the force of the water, and may overlook or disregard the warnings. The danger areas are marked and should be heeded.

As you leave the protection of the walls of the locks and exit up river or down, watch for winds. Be prepared for any sudden gust.

In addition to being aware of the boating variables that are special to the inland waterway, observe the standard "rules of the road." Using these with care and courtesy will help make your cruise more pleasurable, whether you choose to follow the whole waterway or just experience a part of it.

# Sport Fishing
# on the Inland Waterway

The inland waterway provides many opportunities to combine boating with sport fishing. Anglers with heavy lures or spinners, and fly casters will not have any problem finding the right setting or the right fish.

There are two major groups of fish in the inland waterway. The anadromous group is represented by fish that spend some of their lives at sea and return up river to spawn. The spiny ray or warm water group of fish is resident in the waterway year-round.

The anadromous group presents an exciting array of sport fishing. Included in this group is the white sturgeon, which can reach lengths of up to twenty feet and weights of up to twelve hundred pounds. At the lower end, in terms of size, is the tiny smelt with lengths to six inches and a weight measured in ounces. In between are the prized salmon, steelhead, sea-run cutthroat trout, and shad.

White sturgeon, though usually resident in rivers, are included in this group because they are capable of living in salt water. Sturgeon are descendants of an ancient group of fish. They have cartilagineous skeletons. While reaching an extreme size, only those from three feet to six feet can be kept. They are bottom feeders. Sturgeon below Bonneville Dam may live part of their lives at sea while those above the dams have become landlocked. Sturgeon may be fished year-round along the full length of the waterway, but the best period is late fall through early spring.

Two species of salmon provide action for rod and reelers along the waterway. The Chinook salmon is the recognized king of the salmon fishery. This fish has the forked tail characteristic of salmon as opposed to the square tail of steelhead trout. Chinook can be distinguished from other species by black gums at the base of the teeth and by black spots on the dorsal fin. Chinook weigh from eight to fifty pounds. They are usually four years old when returning to spawn. In the lower Columbia the spring migration extends from late February through May with the peak in April. The fall run enters the Columbia in late July and peaks around September. In the Snake River the best Chinook fishing occurs in July with good fishing in May and September.

Coho salmon (or silver) are smaller than the Chinook. They weigh from six to fourteen pounds. They have a forked tail but no spots on the dorsal fin, and the gums are almost white. Coho usually return to spawn when they are three years old. They begin showing in mid-summer and can be fished through late fall, regulations allowing. October is often the best month.

Jack salmon, both Chinook and Coho, are male fish that mature early and return to spawn after one year at sea. These salmon are smaller than their later maturing counterparts and are apt to be caught along with the older fish as their migrations intersect.

Steelhead are a sea-run rainbow trout. This fish has a square tail, and its head is rounder and shorter than a salmon's. Steelhead average seven to ten pounds though some reach thirty-two pounds in the Snake River. They normally return from the sea as three- or four-year old fish during winter or summer runs. The winter run occurs from December through March. The main summer migration occurs from June through August. There is good fishing on the lower Columbia during this period and excellent fishing on the Snake through the fall and early winter.

The once great runs of salmon and steelhead have declined significantly. Land use changes have affected spawning areas and dams have impeded the natural migrations. In 1920 there were thirty-six million pounds of salmon and steelhead harvested. In 1980 the harvest was only about seven million pounds. The preservation and enhancement of the runs have become costly and complex.

The decline in runs can be attributed, in part, to a number of other known factors. Despite fish ladders designed to assist the fish in their upstream travels, young fish may have a troublesome migration to the sea. Some are cut to pieces by the blades of turbine generators. Some die of nitrogen saturation in the water at the base of spillways, where compressed air bubbles literally cause the bends in little fish. Injured or weakened fish become food for predators.

Anadromous fish biology, though well studied, is not fully understood, and the size of returning migrations also can be influenced by survival rates at sea and world climatic changes that effect water temperatures in the North Pacific. The government agencies that manage these resources also deal with the domestic and international politics surrounding them. These include the confusion of laws and conflicts between sport, commercial, and Native American Indian fishing rights.

Efforts to improve salmon and steelhead runs have focused on hatchery rearing of young fish as well as protection of juveniles on their way downstream. Elaborate and expensive screen systems designed to divert young fish away from generators and spillways are being installed and tested. Young fish are collected and trucked or barged to a point below Bonneville Dam. Counts of returning fish are now beginning to show positive results from these efforts.

Sea-run cutthroat trout, another fish in the anadromous group, has a life cycle similar to the steelhead. This fish has a square troutlike tail and red slash marks under both sides of the jaw. Sea-run cutthroat usually weigh one to three pounds, but some reach four pounds. They begin to appear in large numbers in July or August and peak in late September and October. Good cutthroat fishing can be found along the islands in the estuary of the lower Columbia.

Shad are the largest fish in the herring family. They weigh up to four pounds. Unlike salmon, they do not die after spawning, and unlike the other anadromous fish in the inland waterway, they are not native. Shad were introduced into the Columbia from the east coast of North America in 1886. June is the best time to catch shad. They can be found mainly in the Columbia below Bonneville Dam.

Smelt, the smallest of the anadromous group of fish, are usually three years old when they return from the sea. Their run is unpredictable, but usually occurs sometime in the first three months of the year. Indians once used their oily bodies as candles. Today, smelt dipping with long-handled nets from either boats or the shore provide a social gathering for family and friends along the Columbia's major tributaries west of Bonneville Dam.

The spiny ray group, distinguished by the sharp spines on the dorsal and anal fins, is represented by three different families: perch, sunfish, and catfish. All of the spiny ray fish have been introduced from eastern North America. Regulations allow these fish to be taken year-round, but the best fishing is in the warmer months when the water is warm and the barometer high.

There are two kinds of perch to be caught in the waterway. The yellow perch is shaped like a trout and is grassy green or yellow in color with a series of darkened vertical bars along the side. Some weighing more than one pound have been taken. The walleye or pike perch is a dark olive color with mottled brassy specks. They are good fighters. Walleyes average two to four pounds with some growing as large as twelve pounds. There is good walleye fishing above John Day Dam.

Several kinds of sunfish are found in the inland waterway. The most sought after is the largemouth bass. This fish has a dark green back with greenish silver sides. In fish over six inches, the mouth extends behind the back margin of the eye. Largemouth prefer weedy bottoms. Fish in the two to six pound range are common and are considered excellent eating.

The smallmouth bass, also a sunfish, are very popular on the Snake River. They are dark green to pale olive brown. The mouth does not extend behind the eye. They are usually under three pounds in weight. They prefer gravelly bottoms.

Crappie, another of the sunfish family, are also found in the waterway. White crappie are the most common. These fish are silvery with dark bands extending down from the back. They are taken mostly from sloughs or backwaters. Some reach five pounds in weight. Black crappie are less common and seldom grow large.

Other kinds of sunfish are the bluegill and pumpkinseed. The former fish has a blue-black gill flap and a bluish gill cover. The pumpkinseed is bluish olive in color with orange spots on the side and orange and blue streaks on the cheeks. Both fish are flat and oval. They are usually up to about eight inches in length though some to twelve inches have been caught. They offer good sport for children.

Five species of catfish are found in the Columbia and Snake rivers. The blue catfish is the largest. It is slate grey above and white below and can weigh over one hundred pounds, though none of that size has been taken in this river system. The smaller channel catfish are slate grey and usually have many dark spots over the body. Channel cats over twenty pounds have been taken.

Brown, black, and yellow bullhead are recognized by their scaleless bodies, whiskers on the chin and head, and a sharp spine on the dorsal and pectoral fins. Bullhead are not large, though some weighing up to four pounds have been caught.

Washington's sport fishing regulations for spiny rays, steelhead, and cutthroat trout are published by the Department of Game. The Washington State Department of Fisheries regulates sport fishing for the anadromous group except steelhead and cutthroat. In Oregon, the Oregon Department of Fish and Wildlife provides sport regulations for both groups of fish. By agreement between the two states, either a Washington or an Oregon license may be used while fishing in that part of the Columbia where the river is the boundary between the two states. Bank fishing, however, requires a license from the appropriate state.

Copies of the regulations, licenses, and punch cards, if required, can be obtained at sporting stores and marinas located along the waterway. Here you can also obtain information about the regulations and seasons and gain local knowledge on good fishing spots and the most effective lures. Your fellow boaters along the waterway can also be helpful. But remember, they probably will not give away their favorite spots. You will have to discover your own.

# Cruises

**Exploration Holidays and Cruises**
**1500 Metropolitan Park Building**
**Seattle, Washington 98101**
**phone: 1-800-426-0600**

The longest cruise on the Columbia and Snake rivers' inland waterway is offered by Exploration and Holiday Cruises. From May to October the eighty-passenger vessel *M.V. Pacific Northwest Explorer,* leaves Portland, sails down to Astoria, then sails up river to Lewiston, Idaho, and back to Portland. On the seven-day trip the vessel stops to visit historic places along the waterway.

*The Rose*
**Oregon Steam Navigation Company**
**1406 Jantzen Beach**
**Suite 16**
**Portland, Oregon 97246**
**phone: (503) 286-0891**

*The Rose,* a small replica of a sternwheeler, sails short excursions along the Willamette River past Portland's harbor and through downtown Portland, It is also available for chartered cruises.

**The Sternwheeler *Columbia Gorge***
**Cascade Locks phone: (503) 223-3928**
**Portland, Oregon phone: (503) 347-8427**

The *Columbia Gorge* is a replica of the early-day sternwheelers that stroked the waters of the Columbia and Snake rivers. In the summer it sails on the Columbia River above Bonneville Dam. Three, two-hour cruises are available daily from Cascade Locks, Stevenson, and Bonneville Dam. In the winter and spring the vessel is moved down river where it sails on harbor and waterfront tours along the Willamette River in Portland.

**Yachts-O-Fun Cruises, Inc.**
**5215 North Emerson Drive**
**Portland, Oregon 97217**
**phone: (503) 289-6665**

Sight-seeing tours, dinner and Sunday brunch cruises, and chartered cruises are available on the *Yachts-O-Fun,* a fifty-seven-foot motor vessel. Depending on the cruise, the vessel sails up the Columbia River to Multnomah Falls, up the Willamette to Portland, or on special cruises to Hood River. It sails year-round.

# Bed and Breakfast

## Columbia Gorge

### The Dalles, Oregon

Riverview
2325 East Ninth
phone: (503) 296-2793

### Mosier, Oregon

Tara Lodging
Third and Center Street
phone: (503) 354-2410

### Hood River, Oregon

Driftwood House
906 Cascade Street
phone: (503) 386-4591

Truax Inn
970 Cascade Street
phone: (503) 386-2316

### Bingen, Washington

The Grand Old House
State Highway 14 (main
   street through town)
phone: (509) 493-2838

### White Salmon, Washington

Inn of the White Salmon
172 Jewett
phone: (509) 493-2335

Orchard Hill Inn
Oak Ridge Road
phone: (509) 493-3024

## Lower Columbia River

### Westport, Oregon

King Salmon Lodge
Toll-Ferry Road
phone: (503) 455-2400

### Seaview, Washington

Shelburne Inn and Restaurant
Inn phone: (206) 642-2442
Restaurant phone:
   (206) 642-4142

# Further Reading

Allen, John Eliot. *The Magnificent Gateway*. Forest Grove, Or.: Timber Press, 1979.

Attwell, Jim. *Columbia River Gorge History*. Vol. 2. Skamania, Wash.: Tahlkie Books, 1975.

Calhoun, Bruce. *Northwest Passages: A Collection of Pacific Northwest Cruising Stories*. San Francisco, Calif.: Miller Freeman, 1969.

Coues, Elliott. *The History of the Lewis and Clark Expedition*. 3 vols. New York: Dover Publications, Inc. (This is a reprint of the original volumes published in 1893 by Francis P. Harper.)

Donaldson, I. J. and Cramer, F. K. *Fishwheels on the Columbia River*. Portland, Or.: Binfords and Mort, 1971.

Gulick, Bill. *Snake River Country*. Caldwell, Id.: Caxton Printers, 1971.

Holbrook, Stewart. *The Columbia*. New York: Rinehart Co., 1956.

Jones, Stan. *Washington State Fishing Guide-Sixth Edition*. Seattle, Wash.: Stan Jones Publishing, Inc. 1984.

Majors, Harry M. *Exploring Washington*. Holland, Mich.: Van Winkle, 1975.

Mills, Randalls V. *Stern-Wheelers Up Columbia: A Century of Steamboating in the Oregon Country*. Lincoln, Neb.: University of Nebraska Press, 1947; Bison Book, 1977.

Morgan, Murray. *The Columbia—Powerhouse of the West*. Seattle, Wash.: Superior Publishing Co., 1949.

Ruby, R. H., and Brown, J. A. *Ferryboats on the Columbia River: Including the Bridges and Dams*. Seattle, Wash.: Superior Publishing Co., 1974.

Strong, Emory. *Stone Age on the Columbia River*. 2nd ed. Portland, Or.: Binfords and Mort, 1967.

Tate, William H. *A Mariner's Guide to the Rules of the Road*. Annapolis, Md.: Naval Institute Press, 1976.

*United States Coast Pilot #7*, Pacific Coast: California, Oregon, Washington, and Hawaii. U.S. Department of Commerce, National Oceanic and Atmospheric Administration, National Ocean Survey, June, 1979. Washington D.C.

Williams, Chuck. *Bridge of the Gods, Mountains of Fire: A Return to the*

*Columbia Gorge.* White Salmon, Wash., Petaluma, Cal.: Elephant Mountain Arts; New York, N.Y., San Francisco, Cal.: Friends of the Earth, 1980.

# Other Books from
# Pacific Search Press

*An Illustrated Guide to Making Oriental Rugs* by Gordon W. Scott
*Journey to the High Southwest: A Traveler's Guide* (2d Ed. Revised)
      by Robert L. Casey
*Marine Mammals of Eastern North Pacific and Arctic Waters*
      edited by Delphine Haley
*One Potato, Two Potato: A Cookbook* by Constance Bollen and
      Marlene Blessing
*Patterns for Tapestry Weaving: Projects and Techniques* by Nancy Harvey
*The Pike Place Market: People, Politics, and Produce*
      by Alice Shorett and Murray Morgan
*A Practical Guide to Independent Living for Older People*
      by Alice H. Phillips and Caryl K. Roman
*River Runners' Recipes* by Patricia Chambers
*The Salmon Cookbook* by Jerry Dennon
*Seabirds of Eastern North Pacific and Arctic Waters*
      edited by Delphine Haley
*Seattle* Photography by David Barnes
*Shellfish Cookery: Absolutely Delicious Recipes from the West Coast*
      by John Doerper
*Spinning and Weaving with Wool* by Paula Simmons
*Starchild & Holahan's Seafood Cookbook* by Adam Starchild and
      James Holahan
*They Tried to Cut It All* by Edwin Van Syckle
*The White-Water River Book: A Guide to Techniques, Equipment, Camping,
      and Safety* by Ron Watters/Robert Winslow, photography
*Whitewater Trips for Kayakers, Canoeists and Rafters on Vancouver Island*
      by Betty Pratt-Johnson
*Wild Mushroom Recipes* by the Puget Sound Mycological Society
*The Zucchini Cookbook* (3d Ed. Revised & Enlarged)
      by Paula Simmons